My Year
On the Inside

Creating Catalysts for Change

MERIKAY HUNT TILLMAN, M.S.

DEDICATION

This book is dedicated to key people in my life that have influenced my past, my present and will continue to influence my future. To my grandmother, Freda Hunt of Burton, West Virginia who taught me to be courageous. Her passion for life and quest to help others were a constant reminder to give it your all....no matter what. I also would like to thank my children – Melinda, Harrison & Emma Freda whom are by far my biggest blessings and my biggest challenges. There is no instruction manual for being a parent. Thank you for giving me grace when I turn into mommy monster, loving each other even when you drive each other crazy and for your generous spirits. Thank you to each of you for teaching me daily how to be a better person. This book is also dedicated to my sister, Allison, a registered nurse, who endured my endless phone calls during my year on the inside to purge thoughts and seek wisdom. Finally, to all the people who work in our hospitals and care for each other, their patients and their families
– THANK YOU.

CONTENTS

ACKNOWLEDGMENTS

God, thank You for always loving me no matter what! Thank You for giving me a foundation of faith to stand on to help me be strong when I felt weak. Thank You for Your forgiveness and encouragement and for those divine moments that spoke to me and told me I was where You wanted me to be. Thank you to Dale Carnegie Training® for teaching me to continuously stretch my comfort zone. Thank you to Jack Canfield's book, Success Principles that inspired me several years ago on a mission trip when I read "take 100% responsibility for every area of your life." Thank you to my friend Bill D. and colleague Shane R. who listened and advised me on those Monday morning phone calls. Thank you to Lara S. and Kelsey T. – our dynamic team in the Department of Patient and Family Experience. Each of you gave me fuel during the tough times, listened without judgment, stepped up when needed and helped me to be a better leader. Thank you to Sue C., my internal advisor who pushed me to think more strategically - your passion for the patient experience was inspiring. Thank you to Barry S. for your dedication to the emergency department team members and to the patient experience. Thank you to all the caregivers - past, present and future - that walk the halls of our hospitals, you are a blessing, you are valued and you are appreciated.

1 LEAP OF FAITH

Live your beliefs and you can turn the world around.
-Henry David Thoreau

Background

In the spring of 2012 I was driving back to my home office in Greensboro, NC from Burlington, about a thirty minute commute, and I was thinking about the speech I had just delivered to over eighty business professionals. I encouraged them to look at their work life and take an inventory of things they loved about their work and things that were difficult. The goal was to make sure that 80% of what they did every day was in the JOY category, and 20% fell into the CHALLENGE or CRAP category. Well, I realized on that stretch of Highway 40 that *I* had more in the CHALLENGE/CRAP category than I wanted and it was time to make a change. So that night I said a prayer: "God, you know what I'm good at. There's got to be a way I can do what I enjoy and what I'm good at and not be so frustrated every month."

Two days later I had lunch with a vice-president of a local hospital, telling her my story about re-launching my speaking and consulting business and that it was time for me to step out of my sales role for Dale Carnegie Training®. She was a former client for whom I had conducted a teambuilding retreat for her department shortly after she arrived from a hospital outside North Carolina a few years earlier. I also worked with her husband who was transitioning in his career, and helped her son with some coaching sessions as he explored his future career. Mid-salad she said, "Why don't you apply for the new position we have in Patient Experience?" She went on to share that there had been several applicants, none of them with my background. I thought about it for a second and then asked, "Would they let me do it part time?" She said, "No, it's a full time position."

So after six weeks of conference calls, meetings and negotiations, I started part time for the first eight weeks at "Lower Ridge Hospital or LRH (the name has been changed to protect the innocent and the guilty) so I could transfer my Dale Carnegie® clients to a colleague and finish commitments with current clients. In July of 2012 I became the Patient Experience Coach – a title I pitched to my VP because I thought it would connect to people in a more meaningful way. Little did I know that that several of the employees I met in my first thirty days had a negative perception of 'coaching' because of how they had received 'coaching' over the years. They did not look at coaching in a positive light – it had always been punitive. Yikes!

My personal goal during this time of transition was to continue speaking once per quarter to organizations and associations throughout the United States on topics of success, communications and team effectiveness. And that is where this story about Creating Catalysts for Change begins. Here's the deal – this book is about some things I got right and some things I got wrong during my year on the inside. Some things I knew to do and didn't; some things I did when I shouldn't have; some things I knew to avoid and some things I didn't; some things I jumped in with both feet and some things I ran from as FAST as I could in the other direction.

My heart has always been in healthcare. When I was in high school, I used to fill in at my father's periodontal practice when his assistant was sick or on vacation. I found the work fascinating and loved feeling like we were helping people. As my independent nature continued to develop, I longed to work away from the family business and I heard that a new Chi Chi's Mexican Restaurant was being built. I drove up in my AMC Pacer – yes, that was my first car, so cheers to all those readers who started out in a Gremlin, Pinto or Pacer! I found the trailer on the construction site that had a "hiring" sign on the door, walked in and applied for a job. I remember sitting in the car being very nervous and thinking, "MK, you can do this. Get out of your car, walk in and just see what happens."

Never underestimate the power of self-talk; you need to be careful what you are telling yourself. Researchers say we have between 2,000-3,000 thoughts per day. WOW!! What if we are thinking or saying positive, powerful, purposeful messages to ourselves that we believe? What if we are saying negative, demeaning, critical messages to ourselves that we believe?

Have you ever been really scared to do something and somehow found the courage to tell yourself to do it anyway?

Chi Chi's Mexican Restaurant was where I caught the 'restaurant fever' at age sixteen, working as a hostess. A few years later I worked for food services on campus while attending the University of North Carolina at Chapel Hill and followed that by working as a waitress and then assistant manager for a Carrboro favorite, Tiajuana Fats, near campus. After visiting a friend in Charleston, South Carolina, who was in culinary school, I thought my dream was to own a restaurant that floated on the water….OK, so you gotta start somewhere with your career dreams! My father's dream was for me to take over his dental practice. Since my sister had decided to pursue nursing school and had a strong aversion against working with teeth, he hoped I would be his successor. That was not going to be my path….at least I didn't THINK it would be my path.

After graduation (I actually photocopied my diploma and gave it to my dad for Christmas in 1988 because I didn't think he believed I actually finished my degree), I realized a career as a dentist was out of reach because of my aversion to chemistry and math. Several of my friends were staying in Chapel Hill and I knew that would not work for me, so I landed a job as an assistant manager for ….let's call it Orangebee's Neighborhood Bar & Grill… training in Greenville, South Carolina. I was first placed in a store in Spartanburg. I was young, fresh out of school, unattached and loved the coast, so I requested a location by the water. This chain had four stores up and down the east coast, so I knew my chances were pretty good. I had no idea they would eventually transfer me all the way to Ft. Meyers Florida. I packed up my mom's '81 Mustang (a long way from my AMC Pacer days) and drove the long haul to Florida with my cat. The next day I found an apartment on a beautiful canal and thought I was in heaven.

When I arrived at the Florida store location, one of the managers came up to me and said, "There's a guy in the kitchen who doesn't like women in leadership positions. I don't think you guys are gonna get along." You see, I was the youngest manager for Orangebee's at the time and also a female and a college graduate – not a good combination, according to this guy. Well, I ended up marrying him – booyaaahhh!

During my time as an assistant manager for this company, I realized that knowing your job well is not enough. If you can't get along well with people, you won't be successful. If you want to have a triple threat in business today, you need to have the winning combination of skill, attitude and knowledge.

The restaurant company I was working for had a turnover rate over 200%. They forgot to mention that during the interview and I was too naïve to ask. I eventually became a part of that statistic and relocated back to North Carolina to settle in Raleigh. The good news about being fired from that job is that it helped me realize the importance of soft-skills training, or foundational skills as they should be referred to in the business/healthcare sectors. Their management training program had included inventory control, profit and loss statements, food preparation, liquor laws, policy and procedures, staffing pars for FOH, BOH (front of house, back of house), importance of FIFO (first in, first out), daily/nightly balance sheets, seating charts, and staffing pars, but NOTHING on communication, leadership, interpersonal skills, problem solving, conflict resolution, critical thinking, or team effectiveness.

Effectiveness

There are two types of intelligence needed to be successful in business today and these areas will determine your effectiveness. Intelligence Quotient (IQ) and Emotional Quotient (EQ): Dusty Staub of Staub Leadership International explains it well in this brief video: http://www.youtube.com/watch?v=l0JbpP_u-Tu

The IQ represents pattern recognition, analytical ability, problem solving, book learning, strategy and technical learning. The EQ represents compassion, courage, insight into others and their motivations, self-awareness, values, integrity, caring, and relations. Dr. J. Mansoor a pediatrician for over 35 years said, "A high IQ is no guarantee to success in life. On the other hand, a high EQ is the hallmark of a successful, intelligent, creative, and a resourceful persona." You can Google him, too, to watch a short clip.

Back to my story. Now that I was married and had a little one on the way, my move back to North Carolina would bring me closer to my parents. Deep down I knew I was going to need some major help. This move re-ignited my love for healthcare and, once again, my father encouraged me to pursue dental school. He thought it would be a great career for a mother.

After working in two dental practices in Raleigh, I convinced my father to hire me as his assistant. We were able to move to Greensboro and I spent six more years attending school part-time to raise my GPA and help my chances of getting into dental school. I took enough credit hours for a minor in chemistry, Oh My!, I repeated all my biology courses and MATH courses (that has to be in caps because I still avoid math at all cost). I paid for one very expensive dental admission study course to which I drove from Greensboro to Chapel Hill twice per week for three months. Three dental admission tests later, the dean of UNC-Chapel Hill's dental school still wanted me to take the test again – it seems that my organic chemistry scores still weren't where they needed to be. I stood in the lab area of my father's office and said to the dean on the phone, "If you people don't seem to think I need to be in dental school, then maybe that's not where I'm supposed to be." I hung up the phone, cried a few tears, and then started planning for a new future.

My disappointment of not getting into dental school was overwhelming. I worked through the grief with a Stephen Minister from church and took a leap into a new role as a lab manager for a chemical company. When a friend from high school who held this position was moving to California and told me about the opening, I thought, "Why not put some of my new knowledge of chemistry to good use?" After six months of working by myself in a lab confirming resin formulas and creating new ones for application on fabrics, I found the job to be quite depressing. My role was so uninspiring to me that you will never see it on my resume, CV or my LinkedIn profile. For those scientists out there that find this type of work stimulating, kudos to you! It just wasn't my cup of java.

The chemical company was going through some restructuring, so when I got wind that one of the owners was going to take over the lab, I leaped at the chance to jump ship. I called my father because he had shared with me a few weeks earlier that he was going to make another staff change in the front office. So I went to work for him again, now in a different role.

Transitioning from a dental assistant to a dental receptionist/office manager was a big change. There were so many more responsibilities and more relationship dynamics to navigate. I realized quickly that I was not emotionally prepared for this new role. You see, as a clinician I felt like I was helping people, caring for them, and educating them. At the front desk, I felt like people looked at me like I was just the 'witch that wanted the money'. I was shocked one day when an older patient walked right by the front desk, no eye contact and bolted out the door. I thought, "how rude!"

This new role opened my eyes to the business side of the dental office. I found it fascinating juggling all the aspects of running the front office: keeping the schedule full, confirming appointments, processing account payables and receivables, sending appointment reminders, learning about human resource areas and so much more! After I had spent a couple of years in this role, my father decided to sell his Greensboro practice and focus on working a couple days per week in Southern Pines. He had worked at this practice as a satellite for several years and was ready to work part-time so he could enjoy his farm in Bennett, North Carolina.

I realized that working for the doctor who bought the practice was probably not going to work out for me long term, and that I needed to explore other career options. My father encouraged me to become a dental consultant and wanted me to contact a consultant who had been helping a good friend of his turn his general dentistry practice around. She was at a point where her firm couldn't grow unless she had additional help. My father said, "Look, my practice has never been in the black this consistently, and since you've been here we have done really well." So, maybe I wasn't as bad at math as I thought! By my fourth year of working in his Greensboro practice we had created a collection system to create more cash flow, implemented block scheduling to maximize procedure time, cut back on select supplies to reduce inventory and launched different marketing strategies to build awareness. These changes had steered us in the right direction financially. So I decided to launch my consulting career. I worked with this firm for three years helping dental practices implement collections procedures.

Have you ever had someone ask you a question and it planted a seed in your heart that you never thought possible?

One of my father's patients knew I was transitioning from pursuing dental school and he said, "Have you ever thought of being a chaplain?" I said, "No, why do you ask?" He said, "Well, we have a chaplain program at our hospital and I think you would make a good one." So I enrolled and served three years as an adjunct chaplain for a Greensboro hospital.

During this time a few key people in my life encouraged me to also pursue counseling. So after three more years of school I earned a Master's degree in Human Resource Counseling from North Carolina A&T State University. Now, for those of you that thought you were too old to go back to school, you should be encouraged by the fact that my grandmother, Freda Hunt, earned her teacher's certificate when she was 62. One thing she taught me was that age is just a number.

And, for those of you single parents out there, I say "Go For It!" There is a powerful saying: "If you believe it, you will achieve it." Yes, I was a single mom when I took most of the coursework preparing for dental school. Even though my marriage to "Mr. Columbia" did not work out (he was from Bogota, Columbia and the two things that I loved about our relationship were that he was a soccer player and that I could practice my Spanish), I committed to focus on the positive. I got an awesome kid out of the deal!

For my graduate studies I was required to complete two internships. One was with LRH (where I would eventually have my "year on the inside") and the other was with Dale Carnegie Training®. Every time our Dale Carnegie® team kicked off a Human Relations and Communications program we would ask the audience to identify someone that they thought was successful in business. This could be someone in their church, in their current place of employment, someone that they read about in current events or someone who was long gone. When the successful person was identified, then we asked if they would write down two or three characteristics or qualities this person possessed. The next step was to write the responses on a flip chart, review each one, then ask, "Is this trait a Skill, Knowledge or an Attitude?" I must have done this exercise over 500 times in 13 years and every time nearly 80% of the responses would fall into the category of Attitude, and just 20% into the categories of Skill or Knowledge. *If someone described you as a successful person, what qualities or traits, what would they say about you?*

Attitude

If you are going to be a catalyst of change, you have to inventory your attitude. Nancy Friedman, also known as the Telephone Doctor, shares seven keys for having a GREAT attitude.[1] *So take a moment and ask yourself, how you would rate your attitude right now about your life, your work, your relationships with others?*

1. Your Attitude is Your Choice – No one else can make you have a great attitude but you. So you are totally in control of this factor. You can wake up, smile, and feel this is gonna be a great day. That's your choice. Or, you can wake up and decide it's gonna be a crappy day. Again, your choice.

2. Visualize Success – Those with a great attitude do visualize success. If you watch American Idol as I do, you know each and every one of those kids sees themselves as the winner. They visualize it. Any political candidate running for office sees themselves winning. Whether they do or don't isn't part of visualization. It is, however, the key to how they got where they are. Seeing yourself winning is critical to having a great attitude.

3. Humor, Energy and Enthusiasm – That's another big part of having a great attitude. Without these three magic ingredients it's difficult to keep that great attitude. We need to learn to laugh more, walk and work with energy, and keep our enthusiasm up in all areas. I learned a while back that enthusiasm is contagious. Let's start an epidemic! The root of the word enthusiasm is "entheos," which means "spirit within." So it's up to you!

4. Resist Negative Tendencies – Stay away from those folks who want to bring you down. They're downers. "It's too hot." "It's too cold." "I'm too fat." "I'm too thin." "I hate my hair." The list goes on and on. While others can bring us down with their negativity, if we're negative we will be bringing others down. No one wants to be with people who are constantly down and complaining. Keeping that positive mental attitude is very important.

5. Be a "Whatever It Takes" Person – There's a wonderful poem I memorized years ago and while it's too long to print here, it's called "Somebody Said It Couldn't Be Done." So be a double checker. When you're told it can't be done, take the time to double check and be sure. When you're told something is out of stock, can't be found, or whatever, be a double checker. Be a "whatever it takes" person. It's a thrill to make it happen when someone else doesn't think it can be done.

6. Embrace Change – That's difficult, I know. However, in most cases where there is change, it's for the better. At least try it. And worse case, if it's not better, accepting and embracing change will help your attitude. My dad had a fun saying: "Nancy, the next time you change your mind, get a good one." The key to embracing change is to accept it.

7. Be Grateful for What You Have – There is no room for jealously in a GREAT attitude. We can be envious of something or someone, that's a normal trait. For example, I'm envious of those who can sing. I'm not jealous; just envious. When you're jealous you hold grudges, and when you hold grudges you inhibit your attitude. Be happy for others. Be grateful for what you have. Why wait for a life-altering experience to be thankful for what you do have. It might be too late.

Thank you, Nancy, for your wisdom! For more information, please visit www.nancyfriedman.com.

Attitudes are everything. And they are, indeed, your choice. Not everyone has all seven of the keys previously listed; however, having a few will start your day better. Then work on including them all.

The cool thing about attitude is that no one gives it to you, you give it to yourself. I get fired up about things I'm passionate about. Do you? What are five things that you are passionate about? Spending quality time with my family, growing in my faith, serving others, delivering speeches and coaching for change - those are my top five. Take a few moments now and think to yourself about your top five priorities or passions. Write down your passion/focus areas.

"Your attitude, not your aptitude will determine your altitude."
-Zig Ziglar

Top Five Passions & Focus Areas

1._____

2._____

3._____

4._____

5._____

In the book, <u>18 Minutes</u> by Peter Bregman, the author decided he was going to pick just five focus areas to re-boot his career and life. Of his top five, three were business-related and two were personal: 1-Promote his book; 2-Continue to give excellent service to his existing clients; 3-Recruit new clients like his existing ones; 4-Take care of his mind, body and spirit 5-Spend quality time with his family.

So many professionals tout, "I am an excellent multi-tasker." I admit I used to think this was a terrific trait as well. Unfortunately, multi-tasking is over rated and does not serve people well. Efforts become diluted, work performance suffers, errors increase and your ability to focus is impacted.

When professionals try to juggle too many things at once, relationships can suffer too. This is where the ability to say "no" is empowering. One of the elements in my Stepping Stones to Success program is teaching the audience members how to say no to things in order to stay focused on their passions/priorities/core focus areas. So if we have not invested the time to identify exactly what we want to focus on at this moment in our life or what our true passions are or what our daily, weekly, monthly or yearly priorities are, then we are not going to achieve the results we need to. I struggle with this and every few months and have to step back and evaluate my schedule, especially if I'm feeling overwhelmed.

Here is an example of how you can respond and say "no" effectively. For example, let's say someone has asked you to serve on a committee or take on a volunteer role or give away your time in some way to consult, coach or advise or to take on an additional leadership role within an organization you already volunteer with.

1. Use the person's name
2. Thank them for asking
3. Share that this is not a good time, or is not in alignment with your current priorities or focus, or that this task would take away from your current priorities or focus
4. Wish them well
5. *ONLY OFFER THIS IF YOU MEAN IT*: Ask them to please consider you to help them in the future.

It's amazing to me, but only three short months after I left LRH (more about that later...), my schedule had turned into an Allstate Insurance mayhem commercial! Since I knew one first has to start with saying "no," upon accepting the full time position at the hospital I had surrendered most of my volunteering responsibilities except for serving as co-chair of the ALS walk team for Brigitte's Brigade and serving on the stewardship committee for my church. Streamlining my schedule so I could give 110% of my focus to the hospital was critical.

As I reflect on my schedule now, besides running my business and taking care of my family, I've said yes to probably more than I should have vice president of Triad Networks, Board member for a local non-profit, committee member on Staff Parrish Council, Stewardship committee, marketing committee for National Association of Certified Healthcare Business Consultants, Showcase chair for Carolina's Chapter of National Speaking Association…..get the picture? If we're not careful, our volunteer time can explode and we don't even realize it. I guess I felt like I gave up so much to work full time at the hospital, that I took too much on too quickly after leaving. *Consider giving yourself 24 hours before you make a decision about a volunteer or business opportunity and say yes or no. Make sure you are making the right decision and not taking too much on or not declining something that you were meant to do.*

This is where the application of SMART goals comes into play. As you look at your career or personal goals, ask yourself if they follow these characteristics:

S – Strategic: Are your goals strategic? Do they make sense to you? Will they help you reach your potential, help your team or your organization? Do you have too many of them? Do you need to focus or drill down into three to five goals this year instead of twenty?

M – Measurable: How will you measure your goals? What parameters will be evaluated? What outcomes will tell you that you have succeeded?

A – Attainable: Lose twenty pounds in one week?? Double your sales revenue? Increase your patient satisfaction scores by twenty percent in twenty days? Triple your number of speaking engagements in thirty days? Make sure the bar is not set so high that it serves as a de-motivator.

R – Realistic: This complements being attainable and the key is that the goal has to be important to YOU! Are the corporate goals important to you or your department? People will have no enthusiasm for working on goals that they don't give a flip about. And for you leaders out there, are YOU setting the goals or are you involving your team in setting the goals? There's an old saying, "People support a world they help create." So invite your key people to participate in the goal setting session.

T – Timely or Time Spaced: If it takes 30 days of doing something (or to stop doing something) consistently to create a new behavior, then it must have a 'stick-to-it-ness' factor and the goal should be monitored regularly for at least ninety days. Monitor your goal 30/60/90 and benchmark at 6/12 months. Now it's your turn to identify your goal.

My Goal:_____

Specific:_____

Measurable:_____

Attainable:_____

Realistic:_____

Timely:_____

Ok, if you passed that section and did not write anything down, I hope you'll come back to it soon. Maybe talk to a trusted colleague or personal friend or your loved one. A good friend told me once, "I don't do goals." Well, he has a new sales position with a publishing company and realized that the successful reps were setting goals, following a process, managing their attitudes and staying focused on the right activity. In six months, he was recognized as the second highest revenue producer in North Carolina. He set a goal and "Whabam!" The first step is to identify your target!

Merikay's 7.5 Principles to Create Catalysts for Change
1-Powerful Purpose
2-Engaged People
3-Interpersonal Skills
4-Streamlined Processes
5-Shared Accountability
6-Performance Measurement
7-Effective Communication
7.5-Unlimited Enthusiasm

On a scale of 1-10, with 10 being the highest, rate your organization's adherence to each of these principles.

_____1-Powerful Purpose
_____2-Engaged People
_____3-Interpersonal Skills
_____4-Streamlined Processes
_____5-Shared Accountability
_____6-Performance Measurement
_____7-Effective Communication
_____7.5-Unlimited Enthusiasm

Total score _____.
Where does your organization fall on the following scale?

MK's Scoring :
0-25 (It's Past The Time For Change…Don't Wait Another Minute!)
26-40 (It's A Great Time For Change)
41-55 (Strategic Time For Change)
55-70 (Celebrate and Help Others)

Is your organization ready to be a catalyst for change?

Action Item

Make a list of your joy factor with your career. In one column, write all the things you enjoy about your job; in the other column write all the challenges or crap. How does it look? What do you want to change? What's your first step? How will you hold yourself accountable? Remember to be SMART about your new goals.

Psalm 27:14

Wait patiently for the LORD, Be brave and courageous. Yes, wait patiently for the Lord.

Ask God to guide you as you continue to set new goals.

2 DECIDE AND CONFESS

People unwilling to grow will never reach their full potential.[2]
-John C. Maxwell

Have you ever heard of Joyce Meyer? She is a spicy preacher "and I describe her as spicy because she isn't afraid to tell it like it is. Spicy is also a term I use to describe my youngest child, who can shift from cinnamon to cayenne pepper in a millisecond! In Joyce's book, Living Beyond Your Feelings, one of the stories she shares early in the book is about the impact of attitude. She realized that when she felt good, she rarely shared it, but when she felt "tired and discouraged, she wanted to tell everyone."[3] Joyce realized she needed to make a change. So, here is what she decided to do.

Decision and confession: *I am going to talk about my positive feelings so they will increase, and keep quiet about my negative feelings so they lose their strength.*

When I was given the opportunity to work at LRH, I felt God had called me to this position. When a small group of committed people band together, you can create catalysts for change throughout an organization. What follows is a glimpse of the ride during my year on the inside. My hope and prayer is that it helps you in your journey to be a catalyst for change in your career or personal life.

One of the main training initiatives LRH (Lower Ridge Hospital in case you've forgotten) provided for its managers, directors and vice-presidents was a quarterly Leadership Development Institute. Because of my background in training and development and my passion for speaking, I was so excited to be able to assist with planning and presenting at these events. When two of our senior leaders thought it would be a good idea for some of the other directors, managers and supervisors to present at this meeting, I got a little nervous. The main reason was because there were some terrific people selected who did not have a lot of experience with public speaking. Some had experience but weren't that engaging. I was hopeful I could sell the idea of delivering a presentations coaching session to help give some pointers to help the entire group of speakers perform well.

I always get a bit nervous before I present, but as Mr. Carnegie said, "We don't take the butterflies away, we just teach them to fly in formation."[4] Of the top three things I have EVER done professionally, taking the Dale Carnegie® Course (Effective Human Relations & Communication) was one of my top three. If you are looking for more confidence, to improve your ability to think on your feet, relate to others in a more positive way, conquer stress and improve your ability to lead yourself and others, PLEASE go to www.dalecarnegie.com and enroll in the next session in your area.

In 2000 when I graduated from the Carnegie course, it was a 12-week program which met one night a week for 3½ hours. Now you can take an 8-week class or a three day Immersion program. You will be joining a very powerful list of graduates: Warren Buffet, Harvey Mackay (author of Swim with the Sharks without Being Eaten Alive), Mary Kay Ash (founder, Mary Kay Cosmetics), Anthony Robbins (author, motivational speaker), Zig Ziglar (founder, Ziglar Training Systems), Chuck Norris (actor), Bill Belichick (head coach, New England Patriots), Ann Landers (advice columnist), Emeril Lagasse (chef, TV personality and cookbook author), Lyndon B. Johnson (President of the United States), Orville Redenbacher (founder, Orville Redenbacher Popcorn), Dave Thomas (founder, Wendy's), J.W. Marriott, Jr. (CEO, Marriott Hotels), Lee Iacocca (President, Chrysler Corporation), Joe DiMaggio (New York Yankees legend) Rosalynn Carter (First Lady) and Dr. Sanjay Gupta (neurosurgeon, professor and media personality).

So why did I take the time to list all these famous graduates? Because each one of them is a catalyst for change. Each one of them believed in his or herself enough or their boss believed in them enough to invest in their personal and professional development. My former manager in Dale Carnegie® said he wished he had a dollar for every person that said, "I'll take the next class." He said he could have filled up a stadium with the applications of people that said, "next class."

I was introduced to the idea of Dale Carnegie® in a business group. I didn't even know what or who it was. James, a member of our group, had so much enthusiasm; he was a terrific communicator – clear, concise, confident – and he had a great attitude. I thought, "Man, I gotta work with him!" After the Center for Creative Leadership turned me down for an internship, I asked James if I could intern with him. He said, "Sure and why don't you sell for us too!" Since I didn't really know what that meant, I said, "Sure!"

About two years prior to joining LRH, I had met with their CMO (Chief Medical Officer) who mentioned that he would like to see the hospitalists (physicians employed full time to work with inpatients in the hospital) improve their communication skills. I asked if he would be willing to send a team to a public Dale Carnegie® program? It took about eight months to lock down the deal, but finally a team of four hospitalists and one administrator enrolled in the session. I was not their instructor; my role was to conduct one-on-one interviews with each participant to find out their strengths, share about the program and explore what they would like to achieve by their participation. After completing the course, one of the hospitalists gave this testimonial: "The biggest benefit is improved self confidence in general and specifically speaking in public. I have acquired knowledge about validated/evidence based principles of decision making, team building and effective communication. I am using these principles on a daily basis personally and professionally."

What professional area do you want to see yourself improve in for the future? Why is it important to you personally and professionally? Are you ready to be a catalyst for change in your career?

Since a few of the providers were unable to complete the sessions due to work or personal issues, we offered a second opportunity for participation in one of the three-day Immersion programs for which I was the instructor. I was so impressed with the hospitalists' commitment to the patient, desire to improve communication with the nurses, and overall positive attitude that when the opportunity to work at the hospital was presented to me, I was excited and hoped I could work with the doctors right out of the gate!

One of the goals set for me by my VP and the Planning Department (I was so green in this role, I was grateful people were helping to set these goals for me!) was to improve the patients' overall satisfaction with the hospitalists, as measured by the results of a patient survey. In general, the hospitalists' needed to be able to communicate more effectively with the patients and their families. This meant not just being able to clearly convey diagnoses, care plans, information about medication and tests, and other important clinical information, but also treating the patients and their families with courtesy and respect.

Two key components of goal setting are important for success:

1. Your employees need to play a role in identifying the goals for maximum buy-in. When goals are set for people instead of the people setting the goals, this can negatively impact engagement. Also, make sure that the people are informed about goal setting criteria. Personal goals such as weight loss or running a marathon aren't for professional goals (hard to believe we actually have to spell this out, but I've seen this happen). These are great personal goals, just not great work-related goals.

2. If you have a goal and then are unable to work toward it, they are just worthless words on a piece of paper (or in your computer).

A few weeks after I began working at LRH, the hospitalist administrator who had encouraged me to accept the position left to work as CNO for another hospital. I was asked to wait until another administrator was hired before I could begin a coaching program to improve patient satisfaction. I didn't understand why I had to wait, and I didn't agree with that decision, but at this point I didn't question the directive.

That was a weird moment for me because I had been tasked with a goal and then told I could not work on it. To use a sports analogy, imaging being at soccer practice and your coach saying it's critical for you to improve your corner kicks, but he wants you to, instead, work on trapping the ball until the middle of the season.

So I shifted gears and focused on improving patient satisfaction among nurses in the emergency department. I began conversations with the ED director and asked if I could shadow the ED team one day to understand what they experienced on a daily basis. I also thought it would help me with ideas for ways the staff could interact with the patients differently to have a positive impact on communications and human relations, and to improve the overall patient experience.

Other than an initial walk through the ED with my VP the first week I started, I had not met anyone in the department other than the ED Director. The shadowing session was scheduled for three weeks later. I was so excited to be down there, yet scared, too. I hadn't told people that I get sick easily – in fact, my sister, who is an RN, thought I was nuts for taking this position. She said to me once, "Merikay, when mom was sick you couldn't even be in the room while she was in the hospital! What were you thinking??" Well, I thought the opportunity to work in a hospital to learn and help people improve customer satisfaction would be awesome! I had no idea what was in store for me.

I arrived in the Emergency Department to find the charge nurse that I would be shadowing and I had my notepad and pen handy. I'm sure my eyes were as big as saucers! I tried to keep it together as I walked behind her for nearly two hours. I witnessed great examples of teamwork, efficiency and knowledge being applied in patient care. I also witnessed a disturbing interaction with one of the paramedics. A homeless man was brought in; he was disoriented, dehydrated and his medical report stated he had a seizure on the sidewalk. His head had a gash on it and blood was on his already stained, smelly clothes. I said a quick prayer that I would not get sick and noticed the paramedic tossing the tubing from his IV on the man's chest. He quipped, "Alright, Bud, they'll take it from here."

Now, my immediate reaction was, "Are you serious? What a jerk! I can't believe he is treating this patient that way." I wondered if this patient was his father or his Fire Chief if he would have thrown the tubing on his chest and said, "Alright, Bud". So I followed one of my Coaching Principles:

1. On the first offense, give someone grace.
2. On the second offense, make a mental note.
3. On the third offense, have a sit-down.

So I gave the guy grace.

As I continued to write down notes and observe all the interactions, I noticed that several people were looking at me. I said, "Hello" to as many people as possible, but I was trying not to talk too much and stay out of the way. I have a tendency to talk too much, a characteristic that would come back to haunt me later. It is a good trait for a speaker, coach & consultant, but sometimes you also have to know when to be silent.

During one of my meetings with the Director a few days later she informed me that some of the employees were referring to me as a SPY or tattletale. I gave her a Scooby Doo look with my eyes and forehead scrunched, cocked my head to the side and said, "Errhhuu?" You see, she had failed to inform people that I was going to be shadowing that day, so everyone thought I was in the ED to monitor them and tell on them. How sad on many levels. On one level it was disappointing that no one communicated the purpose of my visit to the team; on another level it was disappointing that these people had that perception. *What perception of someone do you have that you need to change? Is there someone in your life that you need to give grace to or is it time for a sit down to discuss perceptions?*

For over fifteen years I served as a business and healthcare consultant, helping dental teams, physician groups and corporate clients improve their communication skills, human relations, team effectiveness, business processes and leadership ability. Now, I was the spy, the tattletale – it was awkward and uncomfortable. I realized that if you don't communicate the purpose of the engagement, there will be confusion and an opportunity to misinterpret the objective. I admit that when I heard people had that perception of me, I let it hurt my feelings. I also realized that I better "put my big girl panties on and deal with it!" I also assumed that the ED Director would let people know that I would be there and my purpose. You know what ASSUME means. Oh well, another learning lesson.

I made another mistake with one of the ED physicians regarding the placement of his name tag. He had it clipped to the top of his pants, and I thought it wasn't a good place to put a nametag because it was difficult for patients and their family members to see. This is networking 101: nametag placement upper left so it is not covered up when you extend your hand. As a new employee, I didn't want to look at someone's crotch (that was my mother's term, so in memory of you, mom, I'm gonna use it) to figure out their name.

People seemed afraid to ask other people to move their nametag, so I came up with this simple dialogue to help people feel comfortable approaching each other. For example: "Dr. Knowingly, my name is Merikay and I'm the Patient Experience Coach. Would you please move your name tag to the upper part of your jacket – either the left or right - whichever you prefer (this is called a forced choice; I didn't want them to feel like they were being told want to do, but had a choice instead). This will help our patients know who is caring for them and our team members know who is working with them. Thanks so much!"

Now it was time to put this coaching method into practice. I approached two doctors. One of the physicians had been in the Dale Carnegie class and I had met him before. He smiled REAL big! The other physician I had not met yet. When I asked him to move his name tag so people could see it, he said nothing, shook his head and stomped off. His behavior was like a three-year-old being angry that he was told to finish his carrots when he hates carrots.

What I realized is that I had not earned the right in his eyes to ask this question; I had not introduced myself properly, I should have said something to him in private. Now, I didn't think it was a big deal at the time, but judging by his reaction, we didn't get off on the right foot. So the next day I reached out to him.

I called his cell phone, introduced myself, apologized for the interaction, shared what the mission and purpose of the patient experience department was and what key leaders in the organization were expecting from me. I also asked if we could spend some time together getting to know each other so I could learn how to help moving forward. I'm so glad I took this initiative because this particular doctor turned into one of my biggest allies. Working together with him and other key leaders, we were able to implement a pain management protocol, improve patient privacy, and elevate communications among providers and nurses. And it just took a phone call to begin building a relationship. *Who do you need to call today, apologize to and ask for a restart?*

This doc also was open to a shadow session to provide some coaching feedback on ways he could improve his rapport and communications with the patients. I was thrilled when staff members would come up to me in the ED and say how much time he had spent with the patient, that he let a patient hug him, that he smiles more, that he seems to really care more about the patient or that he seems to not be in such a hurry or impatient. All this in a guy who told me once, "MK, I don't do hugs." Sometimes it's the little things in customer service that you need to decide are important and confess that you are willing to try new ways of interacting with people. It just might produce a positive impact on the patient or customer experience.

I am grateful for this physician's humorous emails that kept me going during some dark days. I just have to share part of this one, sent to me after he was a 'no show' for one of our coaching/shadow sessions:

MK to ED Doc - Hi! I must have goofed on my calendar - went to the ED last week and I was told you were off....let me know a few shifts you are working so we can reschedule. Would love to hang on your coat for a bit to learn....

ED Doc to MK - I switched with someone to avoid your judgment as I was feeling overly sensitive last week due to a new self-help book my wife made me read.

Decide that you are going to give someone grace who needs it, confess when things don't go exactly as planned and connect with someone to clear up misunderstandings. Sometimes you may not be given an opportunity to explain a situation or a conversation. *Who have you had a conversation with today, this week or last month that you need to connect with to improve the relationship?*

I decided that to truly understand the dynamics of the ED, I needed to be there on a regular basis. Since so many things can come swinging at you every day, block scheduling helped me stick to a schedule. As you look at your calendar this week, see how block scheduling may help you manage your time better – after all, it's not really time management, it's self-management. We all have twenty-four hours in a day. What we choose to do with it is up to us. Sure, there will be assignments and mandatory meetings, and other commitments. But most professionals that I've been introduced to over the years have some control over their schedule, so make your schedule work for you.

If you consider yourself a morning person, I suggest doing the most difficult tasks or most demanding times during this peak performance zone. If I have a big presentation, I love to be the first one on the agenda! I have been described as dynamic, real, funny, and trusted in my presentations and many organizations know that I will entice a few audience members to get on stage with me and dance to Mandisa's "Morning Song"! So if you are a morning person, use it to your advantage.

Here is an example of block scheduling: at the hospital I would block schedule paperwork (a 20% category – budget, invoices, database management, etc.) in the morning because that is when I was most fresh. I usually targeted Friday because there weren't as many meetings on that day.

I also block scheduled rounding in the hospital departments. Rounding is not about dropping off candy or doing a drive by – it involves purposeful conversations with people. Ask what they enjoy about their work, what challenges or problems they face, what areas need to be addressed (people, processes or equipment), which people need to be recognized. My overall rounding goal was to be in five different departments each week – that is one per day. Sometimes I hit it, sometimes I didn't. If it wasn't on my schedule though, the likelihood of it happening dropped tremendously.

During one of my rounds in the ED, I decided to post inspirational material in the main employee bathroom: funny cartoons and a devotional. If you only have three minutes for a break during a shift, why not read something that will make you laugh or think good thoughts!

I'm grateful for our hospital's leadership orientation process for encouraging me to meet people by visiting different departments and learning what they were responsible for. Since my only experience in the hospital had been as an adjunct chaplain or as a patient, I loved going around and meeting people. I realized I was doing pretty well building relationships and interfacing with different people when the senior director of HR told me before one of the Recognition and Reward meetings that I had met more people in six months than he had in five years. WOW! He needed to get out of his office more!

Email Communication

Do you spend the majority of your time communicating to others inside or outside your organization via email? One area that struck me as odd when I arrived at the hospital was the vast number of people that were cc:ed on emails. I thought, "Why can't you just send it to one person?" Better yet, why not stop by their office and ask them in person? I realize that in an organization of over 2,200 people, stopping by everyone's office, especially if they are on the floor with patients, is virtually impossible. What *is* possible is deciding that, when possible, you will pick up the phone and talk to them in person. Confess to yourself that building relationships is difficult if you are relying solely on email.

It took me a few months to realize that people would 'cc the world,' as I referred to it, because the main recipient in the To: column responded more promptly if their supervisor, manager, director or VP was involved. I admit I used this strategy on at least three occasions when I felt like my request was being ignored. If I was connecting with someone that I did not have an established relationship with I would call first, then send an email. Maybe that was the sales person in me. This person didn't know me, so why should I think he or she would respond to an email first, especially if it's accepted in the culture to avoid responding altogether or wait several days before responding? I had people tell me, "Merikay, she never checks emails," or "You better text her, she won't respond to your email." I found that surprising…are we email averse? Do we use it too much in the organization? Are we so slammed, clogged, and backlogged that we are overwhelmed? Or do we just not give a damn? Who knows? Whatever the reason, decide to get off the computer and pick up the phone or invite someone to lunch or meet in their office or yours.

That's what I did when the new hospitalist administrator FINALLY arrived. I decided to give him one week to settle in, then I called him on the phone and asked if we could get together…IN PERSON!

Here's the deal. You are either comfortable meeting people or not. The only way to get comfortable meeting people in person is to do it more often. Having a process to support you is one way to set yourself up for success. This is one of the strategies we taught people in our hospital's Leadership Development Institute. The pilot program materialized for a team in the finance department after the director decided she wanted to invest in her team and decided that they needed to communicate on a higher level, get along better and improve their work performance.

I recently attended a speech given by Dr. Nido Quebin, president of High Point University, to members and guests of the North Carolina/South Carolina National Speakers Association. Nido said that everyone who works at HPU understands that in order to be successful, they must respond to every email or phone call by sundown on the same day. Way to go! I wish I could say that I do this every day. My personal goal is to respond within twenty-four hours, or if that is not possible, I try to call and apologize if it's been a few days.

What I have learned is that communication comes in many forms and when people model good communication, it gives others a great opportunity to follow good practices. When people are firing off mean spirited emails and cc:ing the world, that gives others poor examples to follow.

Patient Experience Kick-Off

One of the most exciting events that took place during my year on the inside was the hospital-wide kick-off for a renewed commitment to the patient experience. The speakers from the LDI were on deck again to clarify how the hospital is reimbursed for patient care, introduce the new Recognition and Rewards initiatives, stress the importance of the patient- and team-experience, and highlight the new standards of behavior (with funny videos to demonstrate examples of each). The event also featured a personal testimony from our president on the value of customer service, a great video of various team members shown with the song, "Smile" by Kirk Franklin playing in the background, and an inspirational close from our Chief Operating Officer on his personal experience as a patient in our hospital. We played college alma mater fight songs as we introduced each speaker, handed out sweatshirts and t-shirts, and threw stress-balls to the audience from the balloon-decorated stage, all while Jock Jams played over the audio system. Over an eight week period in six different sessions, nearly 2,200 employees participated.

As a reward, they received a personal thank you note and $20 cash for attending. The planning by our marketing department was quite impressive and the Service Team played a huge role in volunteering and helping make the events a great success!

As more and more employees attended these sessions, the emails that were going back and forth were positive, purposeful, and complimentary. I was so encouraged by the momentum and was thrilled that so many of the employees were extremely satisfied with the event. I got to dance to Mandisa's "Morning Song" six different times, giving each group of employees who volunteered to join me on stage a copy of my first book project, <u>Stepping Stones to Success</u>. This book features Jack Canfield, Deepak Chopra, Dr. Denis Waitley, myself and other professionals sharing different strategies for mastering business, life and relationships.

In my five months at the hospital, I had discovered several departments that wanted teambuilding and wanted to see people treat each other better. So part of the focus on my segment was the importance of the team experience. The core values in our organization were teamwork, compassion and integrity, so I challenged the audience to ask themselves at the end of each day or each shift, "Was I a good teammate? Did I act with compassion towards my patient or co-worker and did I work with integrity?" Each of us has our own personal compass that leads us; what we follow is our choice.

One of the Food Services department employees came up to me the next week and said, "Merikay, I was so inspired by your talk. I realized that I had a bad attitude and it was up to me to change it. Thank you so much!" This woman had such a terrific smile, I could not imagine her with a bad attitude. It seems that she was not happy about how the transition of her department had been handled several months earlier and she had let it impact her attitude in a negative way. She decided she needed to be a catalyst for change in her attitude and decided it was time for a new perspective.

I told her I would come to the cafeteria to shadow (after all, my first job after college was in the restaurant business), so I kept to my promise even though it took me a few months. I donned a hairnet, black apron and a big smile and worked the Loaded Potato Bar! I had a partner in crime with me and we laughed, talked and greeted each customer with enthusiasm! One cardiologist walked up to our station and evaluated the food selection – we weren't serving actual baked potatoes, we were serving large, delicious waffle fries with your choice of beef or chicken chili and condiments of scallions, sour cream, shredded cheese, bacon bits, jalapenos, black olives....I'm getting hungry just thinking about it – are you?? Anyway, when Dr. Heartblocker walked up I said, "Hello Dr. Heartblocker, would you like to try our potato bar? Guaranteed to bring you more patients!" He just looked at me with this blank look and promptly said, "Sure" in a low voice with little expression – my buddy and I just chuckled!

Learning to navigate the communication channels in a large organization was challenging at times. I was used to calling someone, scheduling a meeting, providing an agenda, talking, exploring ideas, determining action items and next steps, and rollin' on from there. This is where communication is very important because people who lack confidence, are insecure, feel threatened or are just plain mean may take you out of the communication loop altogether. And if you schedule a meeting and don't include some key people (especially if they are above you on the food chain) be prepared for an email lashing or verbal reprimand– and it will definitely be cc:ed to your direct supervisor.

What's unfortunate about my year on the inside is that sometimes I tried to do too many things, which had a negative impact on some areas of my work performance. I knew better, I just had a hard time setting boundaries. There were so many people to help – both patients and staff. Not having administrative support was a factor and organizational skills is not one of my strong points. That's not a good combination for sure.

Now you may be thinking, Merikay, you sure are giving me some excuses here. No, this was my reality – I was doing the best that I could. Finally our department was able to add a team member whose own plate runneth over. Some days we were both treading water trying to take care of patient needs and support the team members that were taking care of patients.

The Merger

It was an exciting day at our hospital. We were merging with another system and the press were coming to hear from the leaders from the new system and our hospital leaders. I was pumped and couldn't wait! This event was open to everyone at the hospital and community (or at least I thought it was), but when I arrived in the lobby 15 minutes before the gig started, there was no one in the lobby – no one from our hospital leadership to greet the new leaders from the other system. I thought, "Maybe they are all in the back reviewing the agenda and someone will be out shortly."

As the leaders from the other system began arriving, I smiled, shook hands, introductions took place, and excitement was building. One of the new health system leaders began giving me names of people for my VP to contact to be a resource for patient experience, so I feverishly was writing down names and numbers, making sure I didn't miss anything. That's when someone walked up to me and said, "Merikay, I need to see you for a moment." I said sure, excused myself from the conversation, and began thinking, "I wonder what she needs my help with?"

"Merikay, we need you to clear the lobby." I thought, "What?" It hit me completely wrong and as rude. No one from our organization was in the lobby to greet these people and I had been interrupted when someone was giving me great information to help our department, simply because the lobby needed to cleared?

As we used to say in high school – BS! I went about my day, attending meetings, rounding, planning classes, etc. Later that day I called this person, told her how rude I thought that interaction had been, and shared what was happening when she told me she needed to see me. She said her director told her to talk to me, so I called the director. The director said the VP asked her to talk to me, so I called the VP. That's where I got the clear picture. She said, "We just didn't want you asking questions."

This was a defining moment for me. I had to decide to let this rude behavior go and confess that sometimes I don't understand people's motives. Decision and Confession comes in many forms.

The Power of Words

A department direction decided her team needed an opportunity to improve their work performance. Stress levels were high, teamwork was suffering and morale was low. I created a customized six session program for her team and kicked off the first session with an exercise which encouraged participants to focus on positive aspects of their work and personal life. What kinds of things did they want to be doing on a daily basis? What kinds of things did they want to be thinking consistently? How did they see themselves interacting with others? What did they want to accomplish? The assignment was wide open. I just wanted them to focus on language that was positive and purposeful.

One of the participants in this series decided to post her "I Am" statement on her office bulletin board. When I stopped by to visit one day to see how she was doing and ask if there was anything I could help her with, I noticed the multi-colored statement above her computer. I stopped the conversation because I completely lost focus and was moved by her words. I asked if she would send me a copy because I wanted to write my own "I Am" statement. Making some decisions to look at things from a new perspective and confessing where things were getting off track were going to help me continue the quest for creating catalysts for change. *What important decision do you need to make today? What do you need to confess to move forward as a catalyst for change?* Here is her inspiring "I Am" statement:

I AM STRONG
Because I know my Weaknesses

I AM BEAUTIFUL
Because I am aware of my Flaws

I AM FEARLESS
Because I learned to recognize illusion from Real

I AM WISE
Because I learn from my mistakes

I AM A LOVER
Because I have felt hate

And...

I CAN LAUGH
Because I have known sadness -(F.B.)

Action Item

Write your "I Am..." purpose statement. Who are you? What do you want to become? In what areas do you want to be a catalyst for change?

Matthew 5:5

God blesses those who are humble, for they will inherit the whole earth.

Humility is revealed in our decisions and confessions. What decisions and confessions are on your heart?

3 RE-FUEL VS. BURNOUT

Any hurt is worth it that puts us on the path of peace.
-Eugene Peterson

Have you ever run out of gas in your car? A good friend would say, "The gas ran out in the car." I would say, "I ran out of gas." I would look at it like it was my fault I ran out of gas, my friend would look at it like it was the car's fault it ran out of gas. It's funny to me sometimes how differently we look at situations.

I was driving back from a meeting on the South Carolina coast and was on a conference call in the car – I was so engaged in the conversation that I didn't realize the gas needle was nearly on empty. Fortunately I had one of those instruments that told me how many miles were left. A moment of panic set in. Then I looked at my GPS for one of those gas tank symbols that shows where the nearest station is located. Trouble was, I didn't have a clue what was near me because I was on a stretch of highway on which I had not traveled frequently. So I took a chance and pulled off the road. I try to follow a rule that if I exit, I need to be able to see a gas station sign because in the past, I've taken an exit and had to drive several miles to the nearest station. I didn't think I had that much in my tank for a five mile excursion at this point.

I flagged down a truck and the guy driving looked like a local (ball cap, Hardee's cups on the dash, North Carolina plates). I said, "Hey! Do you know where the nearest gas station is?" He said, "Yeah, about two miles up the road on the right." I replied, "Is there any way you would follow me there? I'm low on gas and just not sure I'm gonna make it and my cell battery is dead." Yep, double wammy – I didn't have my phone plugged in on the call. He agreed and followed me to the station.

I only had five bucks cash on me. I'm one of those people that carries limited cash – are you too? Anyhow, I walked up to his truck before I started fueling and noticed he also had a pack of cigarettes on the dash. I said, "Thank you so much for helping me. This is all the cash I have on me, maybe it'll buy you a pack of smokes." He looked at me like I had given him fifty bucks and, with a big smile, said, "Thanks!"

Lots of learning lessons here. I know you are thinking, "Merikay, you need to be more organized, pay more attention, be safer." But sometimes you gotta take a risk. I know stopping a complete stranger in this day and time may not be ideal, but I try very hard to think the best first, to see the good in people first.

Just like my need to pay more attention to when I needed to refuel my car, it's also important that we pay attention to the need to refuel so we avoid burnout. This was a warning I received from several people my first ninety days at the hospital. I am used to gunnin' it at ninety miles an hour. I can't remember a time when I wasn't pedal to the metal, trying to have a packed schedule and be in two places at once.

Even in high school I was involved in tons of activities. I sang in the choir at church, participated in youth group (avoided Sunday School at all cost; it was hard for me to sit still that long and be quiet!), played basketball my senior year, played both travel soccer and Page High School varsity soccer, cheered for the varsity squad, served as treasurer for the school, and joined a few clubs. I just loved being around people, spending time with friends and meeting new people. I share this because if you are used to being involved in a lot of activity then finding quiet time and just relaxing with no agenda may be more difficult for you. Some people are used to rollin' through life at 35 miles per hour, some of us prefer a speed of 90 or above.

A UNC-Chapel Hill professor, (sorry dude, can't give you full credit, because I don't remember your name…didn't write it down) developed an interesting performance theory. His idea was that we are wired as professionals to function daily on a certain speed. As leaders, it is our job to take a 35 mph performer and elevate them to 40 or 45 mph. They may NEVER be able to go 90, so why put unrealistic expectations on people? For the 90 mph performers, if we could get them to 95 or 100 mph on occasion – well done! The problem lies when the 90 mph is going 100 mph continually and never lets his/her foot off the gas. That's when burnout happens. And if the 30 mph performer is in a role that requires 50 or 50 mph – they will never succeed.

In a meeting with our COO, I shared that we had a lot of great people who seemed to be put in positions that exceeded their abilities. Some were promoted because of the initials after their name or their years of service, and put into leadership or management positions without any leadership or management training. I didn't think we had set these people up for success. I was concerned that if they weren't given an opportunity and held accountable to develop in some key areas, they would fail and their departments would continue to suffer.

The COO looked at me and said, "Merikay, that's the Peter Principle." Well, I had no clue what he was talking about. I just equated it to what I learned from John C. Maxwell in his book, Leadership 101. It's called the 'Law of the Lid'. Certain leaders have a leadership lid and if they are put into a position that exceeds their lid (or ability), they will fail. Also, some leaders max out at their lid and a new leader can take the organization or team to the next level because their lid is higher.

Dick and Maurice (the McDonald Brothers) were good restaurant owners. They understood how to run a business, make their systems efficient, cut costs, and increase profits. They were efficient managers. But they were not leaders. Their thinking patterns clamped a lid down on what they could do and become. At the height of their success, Dick and Maurice found themselves smack-dab against the Law of the Lid.

In 1954, the brothers hooked up with a man named Ray Kroc, who *was* a leader. Kroc had been running a small company he founded which sold machines for making milk shakes. McDonald's was one of his best customers, and as soon as he visited the store, he had a vision for its potential. In his mind he could see the restaurant going nationwide in hundreds of markets. He soon struck a deal with Dick and Maurice, and in 1955 he formed McDonald's System, Inc. – later called the McDonald's Corporation. Leadership ability-or more specifically the lack of leadership ability – was the lid on the McDonald brother's effectiveness.[5]

During my year on the inside I could see that several leaders at all levels of the organization were in positions that exceeded their lid. Some seemed to struggle with effective communication; others appeared to lack assertiveness and decision making ability. Some were just mean people who were horrible leaders.

One manager was so overwhelmed by her work load and the issues with her staff that she was simply paralyzed and unable to perform. During one of our meetings she began to cry, and I felt so sorry for her. She was not equipped to do her job effectively. She had received no formal training in some of the vital areas that would improve her effectiveness: organizational skills, prioritization, leadership, time-management, and communications.

I conducted a forty-five minute "Peak Performance of Teams" workshop for her team in three or four sessions in order to connect with the different staff members on all the shifts. Part of this workshop was a video called "The Power of Teamwork" from Simple Truths, featuring the Blue Angels fighter pilots. You can find it at http://play.simpletruths.com/movie/the-power-of-teamwork/store.(6) I hope you will take a moment to check it out!

If you have never visited the Simple Truths website, I hope you do. There are tons of resources to refuel you, your team and help you avoid burnout. The first Simple Truths video I ever viewed was called The Race. It's about a boy who struggles to run a race and when he meets adversity time and time again, he finds the resolve in himself and through the eyes of his father to go on. Interesting for us, if we will only look more towards our Heavenly Father to help us refuel when we feel burned out.

This is where I got into trouble toward the end of my year on the inside. I drifted into complaining more than encouraging and was more infrequent with my prayer and journaling time than I should have been. I find one of the most impactful strategies to prevent burnout is to spend quality time each day journaling, reading the Bible and other inspirational material, and praying. So each morning I will invest ten minutes before the dog, kids or workday begins to distract me from the task at hand. I sit in our living room and read a passage from an inspirational book and a proverb that coincides with the day of the month. I follow that with entering the date and a nugget from the proverb on one line in my journal and a nugget from the devotional book. Then I end with a prayer. It takes me less time than preparing a meal or a seminar, yet some days I just don't get it done. Why? Because I haven't made it a priority.

I find that when there are multiple gaps in my journal, my life is usually more stressed and I am more prone to burnout. This quiet time of reflection refuels me and gives me the armor I need to protect me from darkness during the day and keep my mind in the light.

Lately I have added the Prayer of Jabez. If you haven't heard of it, it's a wonderful prayer to ask God to bless you and be with you, enlarge your territory, protect you from evil and help you be a blessing to others. That's my summary – here is the actual prayer:

Jabez cried out to the God of Israel, "Oh, that you would bless me and enlarge my territory! Let your hand be with me, and keep me from harm so that I will be free from pain." And God granted his request.
                              -1 Chronicles 4:10 (7)

I have this printed and laminated on my desk and a small card with the prayer on my wallet. I was first introduced to it while visiting family outside of Nashville, Tennessee. On the bedside table I noticed a book by Dr. Bruce Wilkensen called <u>The Prayer of Jabez</u>. Intrigued, I began to read it and as I stole some quiet time away from the family reunion, I found the information to be enlightening.

I have learned over the years that if you make statements and don't truly believe them in your heart, then you are doing just that – making statements. That's why when I'm coaching someone to incorporate affirmations in their daily work or personal life or encouraging someone to recite a mission or vision statement, I stress that these have to be things that you truly believe or they are just words with no meaning. I believe that when we say what we believe, we give ourselves an opportunity for those things to become real. Sprinkle in some prayer power with that and you never know what can happen!

One of the ways I avoid burnout in my speaking and consulting business is by saying this prayer. I would be too overwhelmed with worry if I was trying to run my business without God's help. I would be too scared or fearful of rejection.

Two of my favorite Bible passages are "I can do all things through Christ which strengthens me" and "If God is for us, who can be against us?" There will be people in the world who try to steal your joy, who criticize you and judge you. You have two choices – you can take it personally or let it roll off your shoulders. I struggle at times and take things too personally. I'm constantly working on letting things go.

A sign of professional maturity is to use the incident or feedback as an opportunity to learn or grow – filter the information. Ask yourself what applies, what is irrelevant and what is pure bull. You be the judge. If you are still fretting over it, give it to the Big Guy upstairs and let Him have it for a while.

Let me tell you about a time I prayed and my prayers weren't answered. I became so depressed and felt like a failure. It was awful. I spent six years trying to get into dental school to become a dentist and was anxiously waiting on mail from UNC to see if I had been accepted. This was my third year applying and every day I would walk to the mailbox in great anticipation (just like the old Heinz ketchup commercials). When the rejection letter finally came, I cried and cried, and I was mad at God for a while. I asked for acceptance into dental school, I thought that was what was supposed to be, I thought I had done everything right. I had been prayerful, studious, and dedicated.

Well, that wasn't my path. That wasn't what I was meant to do. That was my will for my life, not God's will. Avoiding burnout and refueling is about getting in the back seat and letting God drive. It's taken me years to give up control and some days when I try to take the wheel back, He reminds me that He is in charge. Not me. *So where are you today? Are you in charge? Are you ready to be a catalyst for change and let God be in charge?*

As I reflect on that time in my life, I am thankful to the dental clients who have said to me, "Merikay, I'm glad you didn't get into dental school, because if you had, you wouldn't be here to help me with my practice." You see, my calling wasn't to *be* a dentist, it was to *help* dentists be catalysts for change by improving their ability to lead, communicate and connect with their team and patients. Because I was willing to stretch my comfort zone and take a risk, I accepted a position to work with a healthcare consulting firm and leave Dale Carnegie (the first time) as a sales consultant.

This opportunity opened up doors to work with physicians and medical teams, an area I had not been exposed to as a dental consultant. I found some of the issues were the same – balancing running the business, managing patient load, communicating effectively with patients and staff, improving the ability to lead the team, resolving conflict among partners and strengthening the business. Similar dynamics, just on a different scale.

Medical practices have more headaches with insurance; dental practices have somewhat insulated themselves more strategically from the handcuffs of the insurance companies. I want to work with healthcare providers who have good people in place, believe in investing in their people and that their team is the future of the practice. I love to help people, but I'm reaching a point in my career that I can't help the team if the doctors are not on board in the first place. Dentists or Physicians.

With managed care, insurance reimbursements (or the lack there of), legislations, Medicare/Medicaid changes, blah, blah, blah....the headaches keep coming in our world of healthcare. What's my call to action here? MORE PHYSICIANS need to get involved in politics to explain to our policy makers what is really needed for the future of healthcare. Ok, I'm off the soap box now.

One of the jokes I would make to people about keeping their cell on all the time was, "Well unless you are a surgeon and you are on call or you have a parent dying, please silence your phone." You see, when my father was diagnosed with amyloidosis and he was in his final stages of life, and when my mom was diagnosed with pancreatic cancer and she was in her final stages, I kept my cell phone on. Period. Didn't care who you were or what you needed from me, I was going to be available. Also, when I am on deck with my kids, my phone is on, you never know what can happen and if they need me, I want to be reachable. I know many of our corporations today have a no personal cell phone policy and I completely get it, but there WILL be times when you need to have it on. There are people that will take advantage of the system and for those people, take the battery out!

I was speaking at a conference and one of the sales guys told me a story about how he had gone to dinner with his boss and the sales rep was on his phone during most of the dinner meeting. The boss reached over the table, took the sales rep's phone, unlocked the battery, put it in his pocket and said, "You'll get that back at the end of the week." A few days later the wife called the boss and thanked him, saying, "Thank you for taking the battery. I have my husband back." *Are you CEO of the universe? Do you need to be attached to electronics constantly or can you give yourself permission to unplug and spend quality time with your family to refuel and avoid burnout?*

One of the most powerful statements that shifted my thinking professionally was written on a sheet of paper that I found in my father's office many years ago. It was created by Sherry Conger, a consultant that he met at one of the Hinman Dental meetings. I hope a part of this poem resonates for you or someone you know.

Perfection vs. Excellence

Perfection is being right.
Excellence is willing to be wrong.
Perfection is fear.
Excellence is taking a risk.
Perfection is anger and frustration.
Excellence is powerful.
Perfection is control.
Excellence is spontaneous.
Perfection is judgment.
Excellence is accepting.
Perfection is taking.
Excellence is giving.
Perfection is doubt.
Excellence is confidence.
Perfection is pressure.
Excellence is natural.
Perfection is the destination.
Excellence is the journey.[8]

When I first read this poem it was an intense gut check moment for me. I realized that I leaned more towards perfection than excellence. Perfection is burnout. Excellence is refueling. WOW!

During my year on the inside I shared this poem at our patient experience kickoff sessions and in every professional development series we conducted at the hospital. One of these sessions was on conquering stress and talk about stress. Working in a hospital can be SUPER stressful. I'm sure you are thinking your business is stressful, too, but in this case we are really talking life and death.

As we come to a close on our burnout or refuel chapter, here are some strategies to help you maintain your enthusiasm, find sanity among the chaos and deal with negative people or situations. Here is a sample burnout index you can access on the web and includes articles of support: http://www.mindtools.com/stress/Brn/BurnoutSelfTest.htm

I participated as if I was still working during my year on the inside at the hospital and scored a 56. The message on the index: **You may be at severe risk of burnout – do something about this urgently.** Not good...

Refuel Strategies:
1. Find quiet time daily for prayer, devotion and journaling.
2. Never argue with an idiot. They will drag you down to their level and whip you with experience. (I heard that on the radio and have no clue who to give the credit to, but I loved it!) Hang around fun people with good energy!!!
3. Give people grace – even if they don't deserve it.
4. Ticked off? Flip a Prayer. (There's a powerful story behind this, but you have to book me as a speaker to hear it live.)
5. Remember, you are not CEO of the universe.
6. Spend quality time with your family.
7. Exercise 20 minutes per day, eat healthy food and stay hydrated. I try to follow the philosophy of Denise Austin – exercise guru. She recommends eating well 80% of the day and splurging 20%.
8. Let go of yesterday, don't worry about tomorrow, LIVE TODAY!
9. Every day find a way to laugh, use your mind and be moved to tears. (former North Carolina State basketball coach Jimmy Valvano)
   https://www.youtube.com/watch?v=HuoVM9nm42E
10. Set your watch/phone/iPad/iPhone to alarm at noon daily to refuel with a positive affirmation or prayer.

Mike Bailey is the senior pastor at Christ United Methodist Church and delivered a sermon series called "Burn Out or Re-Fuel". I thought this was a fitting chapter title because it sums up the power of choice and gives you an opportunity to really think about the activity of the day, week or month. Are you doing things that will cause you to burn out or are you doing things that will help you re-fuel?

Action Item

Identify ways you can refuel on a daily basis. What is causing you to burnout? What do you need to do more of or do less of to avoid burn out?

Judges 6:23, NIV

But the LORD said to him, "Peace! Do not be afraid."

4 GOING UNDERCOVER

May your choices reflect your hopes. Not your fears.
-Nelson Mandela

Have you ever thought about being a secret shopper in your organization and using it as a way to find out the strengths of your team and identifying key focus areas for improvement? Kind of like the television show "Undercover Boss". Wouldn't it be cool to come in as a patient incognito so you could truly experience what your patient experiences?

It had been several months since our patient experience kick off sessions and I was having one of my regular Monday morning meetings with Lisa. We met weekly to discuss highlights from the week before, explore ways we could support each other, strategize on process changes needed or improvements to target for patient and family experience.

Sometimes we would vent frustrations. We tried to keep these to a minimum because one of the principles we focused on in our professional development program was from Dale Carnegie – "Don't criticize, condemn or complain." I do find verbalizing what's on your heart and mind is sometimes better than keeping it in. But it's important that you are not venting over and over again about the same thing – that's crosses into whining mode and I have a strong dislike of the Eeyore personality. You know the type. Gloom and doom everywhere you turn.

Interestingly, last week an oral surgeon contacted me to discuss how one of his partners fits that profile – glass always half empty, continual complainer, puts down other providers in front of patients. Yikes! He may need to take the burnout index and be a catalyst for change in his life and career! We do need to be very careful who we are venting with so that they honor confidentiality. More on that story in chapter nine.

I shared with Lisa, "I feel like I haven't had fun in weeks. Do you want to have some fun today?" She agreed to be my partner and help me go undercover! I dressed up in a patient gown, light blue hair cover for my hair, green socks – you know those awful ones you get in the hospital with the tire tread spots on the bottom to hopefully prevent you from falling so you can't get up? I also wore a blanket – our blankets were a hideous off white color and looked like they were from the movie with Nurse Ratched (I had to let that one go - just didn't have a dog in that fight). Anyhow, I wore Lisa's black, square framed reading glasses which looked like they came from Dollar Tree, and I had another blanket around my shoulders. Lisa fetched a wheelchair and off we went down the hallways.

The goal was to catch people engaging in our new standards of behavior, the ones kicked off at the patient experience sessions. Here is a snapshot of the ones we were going undercover to monitor:

- Safe and Healing Environment: Keep Noise Levels Down – Be mindful of noise level, speak only as loudly as necessary to relay the message
- Customer Focus: Use the 10/5 Rule - make eye contact when someone is within ten feet of me, speak when someone is within five feet of me
- Escort to Destination: Approach customers when they look lost or confused, ask if they need assistance or directions and walk them to their destination
- Use Elevator Etiquette: Do not enter if a patient is on the elevator in a stretcher or wheelchair (this was the fun part!), exit if a patient in a stretcher or wheelchair is waiting to get onto the elevator, always allow others to exit the elevator first.

We started by visiting floor to floor. I was all hunched over in the chair and staff members did a terrific job acknowledging Lisa. At one point she left me in the hallway because she received a call and two or three staff members approached me and said, "Ma'am, may I help you." One person figured out it was me and had this wide eyed look of surprise on her face. I explained what we were doing, thanked her for checking on me and gave her a Hershey's kiss. She laughed, smiled and walked down the hall. I was glad that we could go undercover to catch people doing something right.

The most enjoyable part of this ride was when we actually were inside the elevators. If the team members stepped off when they saw me or if they declined to enter because a patient was being escorted, I would wait until just before the elevator doors would close and throw off the blanket wrapped around me so they could see my cloths and say with a smile, "Way to go! Good job!" Some people were completely taken off guard and the expressions on their faces were priceless!

When the idea to round among the staff and monitor the new standards of behavior was being tossed around and only focus on the good stuff, Lisa shared that was going to be a first for the organization. People, in general, only focused on the negative or what wasn't working in regards to behaviors or processes. Positive reinforcement or encouragement was not part of the culture. When I first heard her say this it made me sad, then I thought that this was one way our Service Team could be a catalyst for change. Only look for the good and catch people doing things right! *Where do you need to spend more time encouraging people, catching them doing things the right way and giving them positive feedback? Do you need to spend less time criticizing yourself or others?*

One way you can share undercover information is by sharing with your team a patient experience letter or verbal testimonial about their experience. A handful of the dental practices I have consulted with over the years would send a patient satisfaction or feedback questionnaire yearly to random patients. This provided an opportunity for the patient to express their views (anonymously if preferred) on their patient experience.

This is a letter created by Sweeney Healthcare and another way you can go undercover by pretending to be a patient and reading this letter to your team. This language can be tweaked to fit your industry.

Dear Caregiver,

Please excuse my bad behavior, I don't usually act like this, but I'm frightened and feel vulnerable.
I read your every facial expression as an indicator of my health-or

bad news.

I listen to everything you say, and every exchange you have with staff members. I think everything I hear is about me.

Don't forget about me or leave me alone for too long-I'm scared!

I'm not only afraid of what will happen to me, but also what I'll see while I'm here.

It's upsetting to me.....

Sincerely,

Your Everyday Patient   Source: Sweeney Healthcare[11]

To view more of this patient letter and order your copy, visit www.patientfears.com.

In my first month at the hospital, the manager of the outpatient rehabilitation department shared this letter with me. She was on fire for the patient experience and I was thrilled to learn from her about strategies she was exploring to improve the patient and family experience. Our department ordered several laminated posters of this patient letter to display throughout the hospital. This served as a reminder of focusing on things from the patient's perspective.

One of the great aspects of hospitals is that they have become more attuned to listening to the voice of their patients. Nearly all hospitals send a post-visit survey to at least a portion, if not all, of their patients. Those who accept Medicare payments are also required to ask specific questions on their survey in order to receive full reimbursement.

Several companies provide the survey service for hospitals, medical practices, and other health care entities. Press Ganey is the organization LCH partnered with to customize patient satisfaction surveys and aggregate the results. I loved that our Strategic Planning department provided a report that listed all the patient survey comments every two weeks so I could quickly identify the pockets of excellence and discern areas that needed help.

During one of my weekly meetings with Lisa, she shared an experience of one of our patients who also happened to be a volunteer for our organization. I was super disappointed that her experience was not positive and that she had chosen to go to another doctor outside our network and had surgery at a different hospital in a nearby city. This was a definite moment for our department to be a catalyst for change.

My first step was to call the patient and hear her story directly. Then I talked to the doctor involved. The initial phone call went something like this: "Dr. Smith, my name is Merikay and I'm the Director of Patient and Family Experience. Do you have a moment? Great! I'm calling because one of the patients you took care of in the emergency room a few weeks ago shared that she did not have a good experience. Would you be willing to meet briefly so I could share with you her feedback? What day works best for you next week?"

I wanted to go ahead and put it out there that the patient's perception of her experience was not good. I didn't go into details with her name, diagnosis, etc. I wanted to do all that in person. Some doc's see so many patients per day, I wasn't sure if he would recall her anyway. What was interesting about this call was that I sensed some sarcasm, frustration and possible burn out on the other end of the phone. His comments just didn't seem like they were coming from someone who was passionate about patient care. The double whammy was that this was my perception from a thirty second phone call, plus the patient had felt like he didn't care when he saw her in the ED.

I met with Dr. Smith and relayed his patient's story. Mrs. Broken Lady arrived in the ED with an injured arm caused by a fall. She was told by Dr. Smith, the orthopedic surgeon on call, that she had a broken arm, would need a splint and should call the office in a week for an appointment. She said that he seemed like he didn't care and brushed her off as unimportant.

Two major things patients in our hospital identified as top priorities in their care: to establish trust with their caregivers and to reduce their anxiety. Well, after the splint was placed, this patient was in tremendous pain and tried to communicate that to her nurse. She didn't know if that amount of pain was normal or not, and she became anxious and frightened. So frightened, in fact, that she had a panic attack and had to have a breathing treatment.

She called the doctor's office on Monday and requested to see another provider instead of Dr. Smith. The receptionist told her, "We can't do that. Once you start with a doctor, you have to stay with that doctor." Not exactly patient-centered care! How unfortunate. This was a missed opportunity and resulted in another poor patient interaction.

When the patient shared her experience in the ED and on the phone with her sister, she recommended seeing a doctor in another nearby city. The patient got an appointment that day and that orthopedic surgeon told the patient she had bone fragments splintered throughout her arm which were causing her pain. She would need surgery ASAP, so it was scheduled for the following day at another hospital. Bummer for her and bummer for our team.

The good news is that Dr. Smith called me back within thirty minutes after our coaching meeting. He had researched Mrs. Broken Lady's files, determined that he and the other provider in his practice could have seen the patient that day and that her request should have been granted to see another doctor in his practice. He also admitted that he had no idea she was in so much pain in the ED after the splint had been placed. He thought everything was ok.

Here's the deal. Even the most educated patients are sometimes scared to ask questions in the hospital or in the doctor's office. As healthcare providers, if we come across as uncaring, arrogant, hurried or dismissive, we are missing the opportunity to connect with the patient on an emotional level. For lots of people, that's a large part of they want – just to feel cared for.

Feeling cared for and valued is what employees want also. The number one reason people leave organizations isn't because of pay and benefits; it's because of lack of appreciation and their relationship with their direct supervisor.

I remember working for hours putting together an Excel spreadsheet documenting over six months of activity I had conducted in our department. It was a detailed summary of different departments I had worked with over an eight month period, including strengths identified, key focus areas for development, program or coaching delivered, targeted outcomes, etc. I emailed it to three of the top leaders in our organization: the president, COO and my VP. No one responded.

Because I am a catalyst for change, I brought up the fact that no one had replied during one of the monthly meetings in which different hospital mid-level leaders came to the Board room to report on status of their department. I looked at the president and said that it was disappointing that I had put this report together and no one responded. If I felt that way, I wondered how many other people in our organization felt ignored or unappreciated because no one took ten seconds to acknowledge an email. Even a "thanks for sending" reply would have been enough.

After one week I decided to send another follow-up email that had more ideas to create catalysts for change by helping develop the team members in the Emergency Department to improve their human relations and communication skills. This time the president of LRH responded via email and I publicly thanked him at the next leadership meeting for responding to that correspondence. *Who do you need to listen to or spend some time with to make them feel important? What message are you sending by not responding to someone on your team?*

Communication with your staff and your patients is crucial. Remember Dr. Smith from the ED? I also sent to him two documents and asked him to consider key communication strategies to help him connect differently to future patients. One of these documents was a worksheet we had created for the hospitalists highlighting a process created by Quint Studer, a leader in patient experience improvement methodology, referred to with the acronym "AIDET," which he refers to as the Five Fundamentals of Patient Communication.

A Acknowledge
I Introduce
D Duration
E Explanation
T Thank You

AIDET can be used anywhere, even at the fast food drive-through window! At what drive-through will you have a consistently great customer experience? In my town, it's Chick-Fil-A at Friendly Shopping Center just two minutes from my house. Hallelujah!

Chick-Fil-A rep: (A and I)
"Hello! Welcome to Chick-Fil-A, this is Mindy how may I serve you?"

MK:
"Good morning! I need three number ones with orange juice and a chicken breakfast burrito please." (My standard order Saturday morning.)

Chick-Fil-A rep: (D and E)
"Okay, that will be $14.32, please drive around to the next window and we'll have that ready for you."

MK: "Wondermous!" (Another meal I didn't have to cook or clean up after!)

Chick-Fil-A rep: (More D and E)
"Your order will be ready in just a minute. We are waiting on the burrito. That will be $14.32. Do you need any condiments with that?"

MK: "I'm all good, thanks."

Chick-Fil-A rep: "Here's your receipt. Thanks and have a good day!" (T)

MK: "Thanks so much!"

She has a big smile, makes eye contact and has a professional appearance dressed in her clean black golf shirt tucked into her pants with a belt. I've been going to this Chick-Fil-A every Saturday regularly since it opened several years ago. I can count on one hand the number of times people have dropped the ball by having personal conversations, being tremendously slow, messing up the order, etc. To me, that is a testament to the leadership of the organization, to the training and development process, and speaks highly of their customer service and employee engagement. These people seem excited to work there, happy in their jobs and to enjoy people. Why do we not always look for the same type of people as we hire new employees in healthcare? Baffling.

I was inspired today when I reconnected with one of the hospitalists to share that I wanted us to stay in touch and that I was re-launching my speaking and consulting company and writing a book. I always called him "Professor" because he was so good at teaching his patients about their care and had some of the highest patient satisfaction scores among our hospitalists. He was also a great professor to me, helping me navigate the politics, giving me ideas to run up the administrative flag pool. I kept asking him to get more involved in leadership aspects of the hospital, but he just wanted to focus on the patients and his family. I admired that in him. I promised to keep his identity confidential as he shared feedback for me to be a catalyst for change about patient throughput, improving the patient and family experience, improving relations between nurses and providers, and so much more. This was his email reply today:

"Hiiiiiiii there,

Great to hear from you and I am happy for you.

My best wishes for your company and I am sure your book is going to come out great. I just love working at the hospital and feel the healing process every single moment.

Off for a week for the personal reasons but all is well. My family is great and I am sure everything is well with you and your family.

Good luck and take care."

Can you just sense this guy's enthusiasm and passion? My favorite part? "I just love working at the hospital and feel the healing process at every single moment." I wish every provider could feel this way daily in their work. I included this email as an affirmation that we all need to surround ourselves with people that are encouragers. There are enough sceptics and critical people who will jump at the chance to tell you it's not possible, or you can't do it, or that will never work or we've tried that before, blah, blah, blah. Make sure you are keeping a "Me" file that contains letters, emails, and cards from people who have encouraged you. Then when you are having a tough moment, you can reflect on all the wonderful feedback from people and use it to re-fuel!

As I previously mentioned, every two weeks I would receive a report from the Strategic Planning department that showed all of the patient comments from their surveys for different areas of the hospital. One comment from an elderly patient in the ED stood out, so I picked up the phone and gave her a call. After hearing her story, although I would normally grant grace on the first offense, I decided to call the physician involved to have a discussion.

The reason I didn't follow my normal protocol of grace, was because this physician was the medical director in charge of ALL the physicians in our system. I thought, if this incident truly happened, and I can help this physician understand his role in what happened, he could be an awesome catalyst for change. I am thankful Dr. Jones was open to a conversation. When he and I met for our brief coaching session, I told him "I don't believe in patient satisfaction, because some patients will never be satisfied despite our best efforts. What our department does believe in is the patient experience. Whether they are right or wrong, it's their experience." I asked if he was willing to hear the perceptions of a patient and explore simple strategies that other providers in the Emergency Department were implementing to improve the patient experience. I'm glad to report that he agreed to listen. *Are you truly listening to your patient or customer about their experience? Are you using it as a catalyst to make positive change in your organization?*

My Experience as a Dental Patient

Have you ever had a root canal? I hope not. I have had three. The last procedure took place in a different office than my previous two appointments. My general dentist, who I trust completely and have known for several years, used to be my father's hygienist. One day I told her I was trying to get into dental school, she said, "Oh, I think I'll do that, too!" Well, she ended up getting in to dental school, becoming an awesome dentist and has also become one of my favorite clients! Anyway, she recommended Dr. Endo and since I knew he used to be colleagues with my father, I thought I'd give him a try. Well, he was wonderful! His staff? Not so much.

Here is a snapshot of my first visit. I arrived at 7:58 a.m. for my 8:00 a.m. appointment. First I performed a smile test. This is when I stand looking at the receptionist and count how long it takes her to look up. In this case, it took about 20 seconds. She was talking with one of her co-workers about an awards show she had seen on TV the night before, so her back was to the front entrance and she didn't see me enter.

I shared my name and she said, " This is your first time here, so I need you to fill out this paperwork." No smile, no welcome. A robotic scripted response, then back to the conversation with the co-worker. So I completed my paperwork and waited about ten minutes. That gave me time to notice that the lobby was pretty clean, there was a large screen TV blaring news that I didn't give two cents about. I try to avoid the news at all cost – it's too depressing. Then the assistant came to the lobby, announced my name and I followed her back. At this point neither employee had introduced themselves to me or really made me feel welcomed and I was a NEW PATIENT!

Maybe they had plenty of patients and didn't really care. Maybe they were so bored with their job that going through the motions and clocking in and out was all that really mattered.

The assistant was thorough and knowledgeable in her documentation and questioning. I was in the dental chair facing the window and she was behind me, so I swung myself around so we would be facing each other. PLEASE make sure you are facing the patient when you are talking to them, if at all possible. You send a message that they are important and you can connect on a deeper level when you are shoulder to shoulder and making eye contact.

The assistant had to do several tests on my tooth which were quite painful. I knew this was part of the deal, but it still hurt. Then, as she put the x-ray film in my mouth it somehow scraped the inside of my lip and it began to bleed. I jumped a bit and then asked for a tissue. The assistant said nothing. I don't think she realized it happened because she was also in Robotica land.

I couldn't take it anymore. I had to say something. "Ms. Robotica, can I share something with you? I wasn't sure if you realized that the x-ray film cut the inside of my lip. I'm not sure if it was the metal part of the holder or what happened. I just wanted you to know." Her reply? "The metal didn't touch your face." I said, "Oh, well, I'm not sure what it was, I do know that the inside of my lip is bleeding and it would've been nice if you would have apologized." There, I said it. Say you are sorry Ms. Robotica, that's all I'm looking for.

When I went back to my dentist after this initial appointment, I shared the feedback about my experience with Dr. Endo's staff and she said, "Yeah, I've heard that before." Catalyst for Change moment.

After a couple of weeks it looked like I was a ringer for a root canal for tooth number three, a molar. I guess since I had been a dental assistant before I kind of knew what to expect, so I think that's why I got kind of anxious. I should have asked for the gas – you can believe me that next time I will, for sure! Instead, I took my iPad with me, inserted my headset and said, "Well, I want this to be a pleasurable experience for you and me."

I had given the staff grace on the first go round. This time I was making notes and taking pictures. I did notice when I went back for my second visit, Ms. Robotica was not my assistant and the staff seemed to huddle in the lab, speaking in soft voices. They were probably discussing the fact that I asked for an apology.

Now Ms. Assembly was taking care of me on this visit and this was the fifth person in the office who didn't introduce herself or use my name. This is one of my pet peeves at LRH during my year on the inside, too. PLEASE use the patient's name. It's one small way we can connect, make the patient feel important, and help them to feel safe and relaxed. Dale Carnegie said, "A person's name, to that person is the sweetest and most important sound in any language."

Back to Ms. Assembly – she left me alone in the chair for several minutes after Dr. Endo gave me so much anesthetic that I thought my throat was closing all together. I could not feel the side of my face and wondered if my face would hang off the floor when I delivered my next keynote speech! For about 60 seconds I freaked out. Then I said a prayer and calmed down before, thankfully, Dr. Endo walked back in the room.

As a former dental assistant, I don't remember ever leaving the patient for long periods of time after the doctor delivered anesthetic. What if the patient had a reaction? What if they needed something? Even though these patients were most likely having periodontal surgery or a gingival graft or a dental implant, the dangers are the same.

The funniest part to me was after the third time his assistant had left an instrument in my mouth, turned her head completely away from me and withdrew her hand attached to the instrument without looking, I thought, "I know what to do!" So when she attempted to extract the x-ray film from my mouth without looking, going through assembly line robotic movements, I bit down hard on the x-ray film so she had to tug at it, look at me, and look at the x-ray film to remove it. Got her!

Now I had already made notes about my dental visit while I was in Dr. Endo's office. That's just how I roll. Sometimes I make the notes to get things out of my heart and head and leave it on the paper. Sometimes I make the notes to do something about it. I was going undercover and this dude didn't even know it. I always try to look for the best first. You need to be careful though, because if you work in an environment that always looks at the dark side first, it may rub off on you!

About two weeks later I called the office, left the doctor a voicemail that my tooth was feeling better, and asked if he was interested in hearing some feedback about my experience. I told him I would be happy to meet for lunch or after work one day. He didn't return my call. Therefore, I won't return either when I need my next root canal.

When I was a dental assistant for my father I brought in one of my daughter's pink Care Bear stuffed animals for one of my patients to hold during the treatment. She was terrified of the dentist and it took her two years to finally decide to have periodontal surgery. I still run into her occasionally around town and she tells me how much she loved my dad. It makes me feel good to know that she felt cared for when she was at our practice.

My dad's staff loved him and his patients loved him. He was kind, gentle, funny and real. After he died, one of his good friends told me these two stories about him. One was about the wife of one of his patients who asked my dad if her husband would be able to eat steak the night of his full mouth surgery? My dad replied, "Darlin' the only steak he's gonna want tonight is the one he wants to drive right through my heart."

When dad was starting his specialty practice in Greensboro, he networked with several of the general dentists to build relationships. Referrals were one of the main sources of new patients, so for a new periodontist in town it was important that he get to know people.

He returned from one of these lunch meetings and called his buddy down the street, who also was a general dentist. "If I have to spend time with jerks like that, I guess I won't have a referral practice," he told his friend. That was one thing I admired about him. He hung around positive people that liked to have fun, work hard and make a difference in the lives of others. You become what you surround yourself with. *Who are you surrounded by?*

Action Item

Find a way to go undercover in your organization to catch people doing things right and identify opportunities to improve the customer, patient or team experience.

Proverbs 11:16

A kindhearted woman gains respect.

5 CLEARING A PATH

The person who sows seeds of kindness enjoys a perpetual feast.
-Author Unknown

Have you ever felt like there were obstacles that prevented you from achieving your goals? One of the obstacles I realized early on during my year on the inside was the number of meetings people were required to attend in our hospital. I would make comments to my VP about this and question how difficult it must be to get anything done. Imagine the challenges people must experience trying to spend quality time with their team or round on the floors when they were required to be in so many back to back meetings all day, I said. It seemed worse for the senior leadership because they had a mandatory meeting every Monday morning and Thursday morning for several hours. Yikes!

The other dilemma was the quality of the meetings. Since I was the new kid on the block I tried to keep my mouth shut (after all, I was new to the hospital system, so what did I know?). All I knew for sure is that when I attended meetings in the past as a consultant or when I was in sales for Dale Carnegie, each meeting had a purpose, a confirmation prior to the meeting, an agenda, and action items followed by a timeline. Meetings started and ended on time and key people were present that could make decisions or take action. Meetings were engaging, pro-active, interesting and sometimes even fun. *Have you ever used the word 'fun' associated with your meetings?*

There was only one meeting I can remember in close to eight years of selling for Dale Carnegie Training® that was definitely NOT fun. I accompanied one of our new sales reps who had been selling part-time for DCT for a few months. She and I had known each other for about three years through working in a network marketing company together called Arbonne. I learned so much about selling strategies through this affiliation and it complemented the Dale Carnegie sales philosophy of building relationships to build business.

Alice and I arrived at the engineering firm and there was a sign on the door: "Welcome, Dale Carnegie Training". WOW, I thought to myself, this was a first!

Alice and I were escorted down the hallway to the president's office. Right away I noticed a North Carolina State University diploma. For those of you that come from a territory with arch rivals, NC State was our arch rival since I was a Carolina girl. North Carolina, that is. My cousin the was quarterback coach at South Carolina and we battle back and forth about who can use the term 'Carolina', so he and I will just have to agree to disagree. There is only one Carolina, G.A., and that is North Carolina!

Ok, back to the story. I refrained from making any comments about NC State. One of the key things we learned in sales training is when you hit the seat, open with business relevancy. No fluff. Save that for the end.

Before we even made it to our seats, the president shook our hands and said, "I'm not buying anything." I thought to myself, "Well, it usually takes two or three meetings to secure a deal anyway, so that's a starting point and at least we know where he stands."

Alice began the questioning process, asking about the current strengths of the organization. She confirmed what she knew about their business, having researched this ahead of time. She asked what the president would like to see for the future of the business.

After about five minutes I sensed this guy was not really taking us seriously as he started to be evasive and I didn't really feel like he was telling the truth. Now, I had been on a gabillion of these meetings before and this was the first time I felt like we had just walked in the lion's den. This was definitely not Mufasa's den from the Lion King – it was more like Scar's place!

More questions followed. What challenges or barriers are keeping your organization from achieving its goals? Do you know what your people think are preventing them from moving to the next level in business success? When he responded to this last question, the sarcasm shone brightly. Now I was in trouble because I could feel myself starting to get frustrated and I wondered if it was showing on my face. One thing that drives me nuts is mean spirited sarcasm.

I could tell by Alice's expression that I was showing my frustration, so I stood up and walked out of the meeting. I didn't say a word, I just got up. I had never done that before in over fifteen years of consulting. And I have had a lot of meetings with a lot of difficult personalities.

At that particular point, I couldn't tell if I was going to cry or start cussing this guy out. I didn't like the way he was treating our new sales rep. He was condescending, rude, sarcastic, plus I felt he was lying. I also wasn't sure if he didn't really give a damn about his team or if didn't feel like we deserved to be treated in a professional manner.

I went to the restroom, tried to get it together, said a prayer and then walked back into the room. When his behavior continued, I couldn't listen anymore. I interrupted the questioning, looked him straight in the eye, called him by name and said, "Mr. Scar, I have been on several meetings in my time with Dale Carnegie training and after we meet with business leaders, we usually go back to our car and say, 'Wow, they've got this going on or this part was impressive. We generally always find something good about the organization, whether we are going to do business together or not. You know what I'm gonna say when I get to my car today with Alice? I'm gonna say, "what an asshole."' (I know that wasn't very Dale Carnegie of me, sorry!) I continued: "I don't think you've been honest with us during this meeting and your sarcasm and rudeness are very demeaning."

Alice looked down at her notepad. I sat with my lip quivering because I was trying not to cry or yell at this guy. A few silent seconds later, the president stood up and came around from behind his huge cherry desk. I thought he was going to slug me or escort us out. Instead, he shut his office door and said, "Ok, spend the next ten minutes telling me how to be less sarcastic." Catalyst for Change moment.

I said, "Dale Carnegie's number one human relation principle is Don't Criticize, Condemn or Complain. So moving forward, if you would make a commitment to follow that one principle, you would be making strides. Also, if you look up the word sarcasm, it means ripping flesh and I don't think it serves you well as the president of this company."

More dialogue followed, and this time I felt he was being real and honest. The wall had come down. He said that he didn't see himself that way but that his wife would be happy that we had this conversation. The good news? He spend several thousand dollars with our organization on training for his people and he actually enrolled in the High Impact Presentations program that I taught a few months later.

The lesson I learned from this encounter is that sometimes you have to clear a path with people. Put it out on the table. You are either moving forward or you aren't, but at least you know where you stand.

I received a hand written note from Mr. Lion (the now tamer version of Mr. Scar). When I called him to thank him personally, he said he had memorized my cell number (not sure if that is a good thing or a bad thing)! I also told him that every time I drive by his building I honk my horn – giving him a shout out of encouragement. He just laughed. Even when you have conflict with someone, if both parties are willing to meet in the middle, you never know what you might accomplish. *Who do you currently have conflict with that you need to clear a path to repair or build a stronger relationship?*

During my year on the inside, one area where I tried to meet two VP's in the middle never worked out. You see, we were planning another Leadership Development Institute and I really wanted Ann from the Planning department to present a program. She was key in helping our employees at the patient experience kickoff sessions understand the financial impact of the Affordable Care Act and how the different government "buckets of reimbursement money" are earned. The two VP's said that they didn't feel she should present and that she came across as condescending to the audience. I knew there were opportunities for her to improve, so I offered to meet with her to discuss different ways to present. They rejected that idea, saying instead, "No, we prefer that her supervisor talk with her about those things."

So instead of sharing the feedback and concerns with Ann, they just deleted her from the agenda all together. She had worked hours putting this presentation together and I was so disappointed that they didn't even tell her why. The VP's never mentioned it to her boss either, so yes, I took the Catalyst for Change opportunity and met with her myself.

Months later we were meeting with a consultant hired to work with our Emergency Department. After discussing ideas and opportunities to improve with Ann, I suggested to the consultant that Ann should present in front of over 100 leaders of the ED. Ann knew her stuff, she had just needed a little guidance on how to present information in a way that connects with the audience.

Ann and I recently co-presented a program at the National Medical Group Managers Association meeting in Las Vegas, to an audience of more than 300. Our collective evaluation score was a 4.83 out of 5.0 – I would say she connected! *Are you giving people on your team feedback on their performance that will help them improve?*

One of my responsibilities at the hospital was to conduct general orientation for new employees and introduce them to the Patient Experience department. I was thrilled when my VP gave me full creative license to shift things up a bit. She cleared a path for me so I was able to pull some of the strengths from her PowerPoint presentation, add a few segments for audience participation and weave in some stories to give the hour more impact.

I remember being so moved when I was going through orientation when the president of LRH told new employees if they found anyone that was not being kind, he wanted to know about it. Then he gave everyone his cell phone number. WOW! I was impressed.

The core values of the organization were teamwork, integrity and compassion. These made such an impact on me that I put them at the end of my email signature and printed a name plate for my door that included those words as well. Of course, later the Marketing department told me I had to change my email signature because it was not the standard tag line they required. Somehow, I kept forgetting to do that.

As I navigated my way through the organization, meeting people in different departments, I made some interesting discoveries. There were definite pockets of excellence throughout the organization and the number of awards and recognitions in certain clinical areas were quite impressive. What was concerning to me was that the elements of teamwork and compassion were missing from several departments.

We had some definite paths to clear. The organization excelled clinically. But what was lacking were soft or foundational skills: communication, human relations, leadership and the fundamental need for people to understand how to treat each other with kindness and respect.

I remember several people making negative comments about our Human Resource department, and that concerned me greatly. I wanted to figure out for myself what all the hype was about, so I connected with one of the key persons that so many people were complaining about. Well, two minutes into the meeting, I saw exactly what these other people had seen. Impressions I received? Arrogant & condescending are two words that come to mind. Observations, not Criticisms. *What first impressions do people get when people meet you or your team members for the first time?*

On one occasion I asked the Senior Director of HR to consider performing a 360-degree assessment of his department to uncover some dynamics that may have been holding the department back. He just looked at me and smiled, with no intention of doing that. Deep down I wondered if it was because it would reflect poorly on multiple people in the department, not just the one employee with whom I had interacted. My moment to be a Catalyst for Change was over. There was nothing I could do and that was disappointing. I was asked to facilitate a small segment for one of their staff meetings, interestingly Ms. Arrogant & Condescending was not present.

As the serenity prayer goes, sometimes you have to realize what you have control over and what you don't. One thing I did have control over was the number of patients I talked to on a daily basis. I made an effort to talk to at least one patient or visitor every day.

One path that was cleared happened on one of my visits to the Emergency Department. There was a man in an overflow bed in the ED hallway. I really hated when people had to be in hall beds, especially when they were facing the entry ways. There was little privacy and it was difficult for the patient to rest with the constant activity. I stopped by his gurney and said, "Hello. I'm sorry you are in a hall bed. Can I get you anything?"

Sometimes I forgot to introduce myself and this was one of those occasions. I knew there wasn't much I could do, but I could get him a blanket or ask the nurse if he could have food or water or check on test results. The patient said, "I just don't feel good. I feel nauseous." I said, "I'm sorry you feel bad. Let me find your nurse and I'll see what we can do. I'll bring a cold cloth for your neck because sometimes that helps."

I went to the nurse's station to see who was in charge of this area and found Ms. Grouchy was on deck. So I approached her and said, "The patient in hall bed G said he is nauseous. Is there anything you can give him? I'm going to get a wet cloth for him." She said, "I wouldn't get him one, he's just going to throw it at you. He doesn't remember me because my hair is shorter now. I took care of him at another hospital I worked for and he was very difficult."

As a Catalyst for Change, I got a wet cloth for him anyway. I told him, "I spoke to your nurse and she will see if there is anything she can get for you." I offered the cloth and again apologized that he wasn't feeling well. He said, "I don't mean to be difficult, I just don't feel well." I said I understood and hoped he felt better soon.

The word jaded comes to mind here. Ms. Grouchy was letting a previous experience dictate the present. I know it's tough sometimes to give people the benefit of the doubt, but we need to. How many times have you looked at a chart and made an assumption about a person based on their condition, background, personality, or other information?

I thought this patient was probably being treated for drug or alcohol addiction and, since I have relatives that have struggled with that for years, I know it can be very difficult to recover from. In fact, my cousin, a successful pharmacist, battled addiction to drugs and alcohol for years. He finally cleared a path and was clean for one year prior to his untimely death. Too much damage had been done to his organs and my cousin found her brother slumped over his computer one morning when he failed to show up to work. I remember getting the call while I was on my first mission trip in Mexico. It stunk I couldn't be with my family. My cousin and I weren't super close, but I was close to his mom and his younger sister. I knew that I couldn't be at the funeral and that made me sad. Sad day for sure.

One path that needs to be cleared in health care and dentistry is making sure everyone on your team knows how to communicate with empathy to their patient. But, it doesn't stop there. We must also have empathy for coworkers on our team as well.

The patient experience will be impacted if your team does not treat each other well. Here is a simple communication tool you can use with your team to help them connect on a deeper level with your patients and also with each other. I call it OREO coaching. You must first envision a scrumptious handful of chocolate and cream cookies sitting next to a full glass of milk. Imagine you are so excited to eat these jewels that you poured the milk so quickly that there are little bubbles at the top.

Okay, now that you have the visual, imagine the top layer of the cookie is something positive and purposeful that you say to your patient or team member. The cream in the middle is the correction, change, encouragement, or information that you want to share. The bottom layer of the cookie is another positive and purposeful statement. Here are a few examples to consider:

Caregiver to Patient

Caregiver: "Ms. Patient, I'm so glad you came in today so we could take care of you. I'm sorry that you are in pain."
(The top layer – positive & purposeful)

Caregiver: "We need to run some tests to figure out exactly what may be going on and take a few x-rays. The radiologist will be in within the hour and then we should have the test results back by 3:00 p.m.
(The middle layer – information)

Caregiver: "We are going to take real good care of you. Please let me know if I can get you anything to make you comfortable."
(The bottom layer – positive & purposeful)

Supervisor to Nurse

Supervisor: "Ms. Nurse, thank you for helping the new nurse assistant orient today on the floor. I think it really helped him feel comfortable.
(The top layer – positive & purposeful)

Supervisor: "One of the patients mentioned they had pressed their call button several times and no one responded for several minutes. Let's make sure that we honor the no pass zone when we see a call light on moving forward.
(The middle layer – correction)

Supervisor: "Thank you so much for your dedication to the patients and also for helping our new team members."
(The bottom layer – positive & purposeful)

Dentist to Scheduling Coordinator

Dentist: "Sarah, one of your strengths is how you talk to the patients. You are so welcoming and inviting and you help them to feel comfortable.
(The top layer – positive & purposeful)

Dentist: "One area that needs to improve is your attention to detail. We had two patients come in this week on my schedule that had appointment cards but were not entered into the computer schedule. If you will make sure the computer entry is done first, prior to writing the appointment card, that should help complete the task correctly."
(The middle layer – process improvement)

Dentist: "Thanks again for all your effort and I know you will be able to improve in this one important area to help the schedule flow well."
(The bottom layer – positive & purposeful)

Some people are just naturally good at communicating. For some, it takes a lot of work to speak clearly and concisely, using good human relation principles. If you have not read How to Win Friends and Influence People by Dale Carnegie, I highly recommend it if you want to clear a path toward having good relationships with others. More on that in chapter eight.

Clearing a path mentally is critical to success. Have you ever thought that some people are just born to worry? Anxietyzone.com states that we were only born with two fears – the fear of heights and loud noises. Isn't it interesting how we learn to become fearful of so many other things? Fear of failure, loss, disappointment, illness, abandonment, etc. I don't want to stay here too long mentally, which is why bringing up the importance of having the right mental attitude can give you an edge in the business environment today.

A few years ago a friend from high school recommended the book The Joy of Living by Youngey Mingyur Rinpoche. This

Buddhist teacher is known as "the happiest man in the world."

For years I used to buy in to the "don't worry, be happy" school of thought. Don't worry about things, man! Just choose to be happy! I wondered why affirmations weren't working for me sometimes and I beat myself up mentally because I would think the worst or have a difficult time pulling myself up out of a slump. I would feel guilty for feeling guilty! That's weird.

I think that is one reason why God brought my husband Jeff into my life. He is so easy going, laid back and relaxed. I'm high strung, intense, enthusiastic about everything, and don't sit still. Over the years I have had to teach myself to relax. Teach myself not to worry. Teach myself that it's ok to have bad thoughts; you just don't want to let the bad thoughts hover too long in your brain. The bad thoughts will come, the key is to let them move on.

Consider this from The Joy of Living: "Positive emotions such as love, compassion, friendship, and loyalty strengthen the mind, build our confidence, and enhance our ability to assist those in need of help. Negative emotions, such as fear, anger, sadness, jealousy, grief, or envy -- often translated as 'non-virtuous' feelings – are emotions that tend to weaken the mind, undermine confidence, and increase fear. More or less neutral feelings, meanwhile, basically consist of ambivalent responses – the kinds of feelings we might have toward a pencil, a piece of paper, or a staple remover. Try as you might, it's hard to feel positively or negatively toward a pencil!" (p. 168 – The Joy of Living)

My year on the inside was challenging at times because my path would cross with people who frequently displayed negative emotions. The negativity was in emails, conversations and during meetings. I know working in healthcare is stressful, I had no idea how depressing the work culture could be at times. In one meeting a VP admitted the negativity to me by saying, "We are so dysfunctional." I wondered if this VP had been at the organization for more than five years, why hadn't she done something about it?

This same VP told me if I needled our president too much, he might decide we don't need a patient experience department. My reply was, "That's okay with me." You see, I knew that to be a Catalyst for Change required risk taking. I had to be willing to put it all on the table and go the extra mile to make change. I realized that working under this VP was impacting my ability to make change, so I began thinking how our department could realign under another leader. More to come on that later.

Listening to the Voice of the Employee

Several employees shared with me that they would appreciate a discount when they ate in the cafeteria. After the fourth or fifth person said this to me, I took it as a sign that I needed to be a Catalyst for Change to see how an employee discount could be possible. I called the Food Services department to find out who I needed to talk with. The call went something like this:

MK: "Mr. Cafeteria? Hi! This is Merikay in Patient Experience. Do you have a few minutes?"   (Asking this question helps you discern if it's a good time to talk or not.)

Mr. C: "Sure, I have a minute."

MK: "Mr. Cafeteria, the reason I'm calling is because a few hospital employees have mentioned to me over the last couple of months how much they would appreciate an employee discount when they eat in the cafeteria. I have no idea if that has ever been offered in the past or what the possibility would be for the future, and thought I would give you a call to see if you would be willing to explore that idea with me?"

Mr. C: "Yeah, let's talk about it."

MK: "Well, I used to be a restaurant manager and I know it's important to cover your food cost and make sure the business is profitable. I'm just wondering how other hospitals handle an employee discount? Would you mind if I called a few other hospitals to see how they do it and then we can reconnect?"

Mr. C: "Yeah, that sound good."

Several weeks passed. I called two other hospitals and found out they do give employee discounts. When I ran into the manager in the Bistro, he said they were looking into it, so I felt hopeful.

A few more months passed and the cafeteria was closed due to some renovations. When they re-opened, it was amazing!

During my year on the inside, one of my goals was to eat in the cafeteria at least once per week so I could connect with various team members. I wanted to say hello, ask how their day was going, how they were doing. Not purposeful rounding, just trying to be inviting and friendly. One of the employees who had originally asked me about the discount came up to me and said, "Well, we got an employee discount, but they jacked the prices up so high, it doesn't really matter." So, while initially I was excited about the discount, when I realized the prices had increased significantly it took a little wind out of the sail.

What was more disturbing is that when I was shadowing in the cafeteria one of the team members who worked there shared that he was the only person on the team with a culinary degree. He indicated he was demoted both in title and in pay for financial reasons, then told by the manager that they needed to raise the cafeteria prices so they could pay off the renovations more quickly. Now, this is not a great way to show appreciation for your employees!

This made me sad and there was nothing I felt I could do about it. I did encourage him to follow his dreams and I hope that he took a job as Food Services Manager for another hospital, or at least that his title and pay were reinstated if he chose to stay at LRH. *What message are you sending to your staff about financial choices you have made in your business?*

One of my dental clients made a commitment early in her practice to not buy any equipment until she had paid off any existing loans. I admired the way she was a good steward of funds, followed a budget and still found a way to implement a bonus system to compensate her employees. There's nothing worse than getting in over your head financially when you are first starting out. Most providers already have debt from medical or dental school and if you have to have the latest, greatest gadgets, the cost will certainly add up over time.

Financial stress is an obstacle that my father dealt with every tax season. It seemed like he would be in a bad mood for about three months every year, March through May. What a bummer! He worked hard all year and then would stress about his tax projection. *What path do you need to clear with your finances to reduce stress?*

Action Item

Examine your household and business budget. Are you operating within your means or are you overextended? Are you paying yourself first and saving money? You can borrow money for college; you can't borrow money for retirement. Do you make charitable contributions? *Consider a thirty day hold on future purchases that exceed a certain amount to see if you really need the latest and greatest thing-a-ma-jig!*

1 Timothy 6:6

Yet true godliness with contentment is itself great wealth.

6 THE BENCH

Just by changing your perspective, you can not only alter your own experience, you can also change the world.
— Yogey Mingyur Rinpoche

Has one of your employees ever had an idea that spread like wildfire? One of the parking attendants at LRH was stationed near the entrance to the Heart Center and the Executive offices. We'll call him Mr. Parking. During my year on the inside, whenever I would walk by him I would smile and say, "Hello!" One day he said, "Do you have a minute? I'd like to make a suggestion." I was already late for a meeting, but I thought "I've walked past this guy several times, now he's asking for a few minutes of my time so I need to give it to him."

He said, "I'm a retired nurse and I've been working here as a parking attendant for a while. I have noticed that a lot of our patients who walk from the parking lot get really winded from the long walk. Also, when they are leaving the building I don't think they really realize how long of a walk it is. So by the time they get to me, they are asking to sit on my stool or are leaning up against the building column. Would it be possible to get a bench so they would have place to sit?" What a Catalyst for Change moment!

"That's a terrific idea!", I said. "Let me look into it and get back to you."

Now, one thing I have realized about myself in my 50 plus years is if I don't write it down, the likelihood of me remembering something drops dramatically. Are you the same way? I used to be in awe of my father when a patient would come in after six or twelve months and he would say, "So how is Jeremy doing in school?" or "Did the wedding go well?" or "How did you and your wife enjoy your vacation in Florida?" I thought, "How in the heck does he remember this stuff?"

I was in my early 20's at the time and had only been working for him a few weeks as his dental assistant when I discovered his secret. He would make notes in the margin on the patient's chart on any new details his patient's shared during their visit, then he would glance over them before he started the exam. I loved that he focused on the patient as an individual first before jumping into the clinical aspect.

The other thing that was great about dad is that he didn't use fancy dental jargon when he talked to the patient. He learned that from one of his instructors on a military base where he served for part of his payback to the government for providing tuition to dental school. This ole' codger (as dad described him) had a set of teeth in a mason jar filled with fluid on the counter by the patient chair. When people wouldn't accept periodontal treatment he would pull that jar down and say, "Well, that's ok, this is your other option." Then Dr. Ole Codger would show 'em the jar with the set of false teeth. The power of visual aids! Two lessons: Write things down and use terms patients/customers understand.

The vision of the benches started coming to life one day when I stopped by the parking attendant and he said, "So, how are we coming on the bench? I mentioned to the president that we were getting benches." A moment of panic set in. I had not looked into it. I hate telling someone I'm going to do something and then not following through.

Since I was standing with my colleague who I refer to as my internal advisor, I asked if she would put a work order in because she was headed back to her office, and she said she would. Electronic work orders were one of the ways we had to request things at LRH. Your request would get ranked, then an automated system would send you an email sharing the ranking and who was going to fulfill the request. Finally, another email would be sent when the request was completed. More emails!

A couple of days later I walked by the attendant again. At least for the past ten times I had walked by him, he had asked about the benches. So I called my internal advisor when I got back to my office and said, "So what's up with the bench idea? Were you able to put the request in?" On the other end of the line I heard "OOOHHH, I forgot!" Been there, done that.

So I began the computerized process of entering the request. Now, here's the deal. My experience with our system had not been super in the past. I had requested the tube stations, similar to those found at a drive-up bank teller, be padded to reduce the noise at the nurses stations when tubes were delivered. I had asked for blinds on the emergency room doors to be repaired. I requested some hospital floors to cleaned, the front entrance to be power washed, and so forth. But it seemed like there was NEVER a timely response of the work order being fulfilled. So I had already learned my lesson that just because you enter this in the system, doesn't mean it will get done.

I had gotten so frustrated with the appearance of the front entrance to the hospital with spilled drinks, gum, cigarette butts, and other trash. In exasperation, I thought I was the only person who cared about the first impression people got when they walked onto our campus. When I voiced my opinion to my VP, she expressed the same sentiment, yet she didn't have much luck getting the walkways cleaned, either. Unacceptable!

I decided to be a Catalyst for Change. I contacted the Director of Plant Operations and asked him to meet me in front of the building so I could explain in person what I was hoping to accomplish by cleaning these walkways. I didn't get too detailed in my meeting request over the phone and via email. Yes, I sent both. If you have a strong connection with people, just an email is fine, if you are still earning the right to do business, then call first and then email)

It was a blustery day and I stood outside with the Mr. Plant Ops telling him about Chick-Fil-A – yes, back to my Saturday morning hang out. Every Saturday at my local Chick-Fil-A they clean the sidewalks. EVERY SATURDAY, rain, shine, snow or wind, an employee attaches a scrub brush to a hose, and uses a pressure washer, a regular broom, water and suds to do the job. This employee has his custom black shoes, pants, shirt, hat and, when it's cold, his black jacket with the Chick-Fil-A logo.

So why has it taken me months to get the damn walkways cleaned, and why has even my VP, who had been there years, been unsuccessful? I laughed one day when she said she was going to come over in her jeans with a bucket and do them herself. I wanted to join her! I wasn't giving up, but I did put it on the back burner so I could focus on getting those benches installed.

Fortunately Mr. Parking RN was also on duty at one of the entrances, so I introduced him to Mr. Plant Ops and he shared the story and his vision for the benches. I could see Mr. Plant Ops thinking. He put his hand on his chin and said, "Well, Merikay, I think we could actually put two benches here. One near the entrance under the covered walkway and then one close to the parking deck." TWO????? He was making my day!

This is where the meeting became meaningful. Mr. Plant Ops said, "You know, I was at Duke University Hospital with my father this year when he had some surgery. He fell while walking to the parking deck. I wonder if there had been a bench there if he probably could've rested and not fallen."

WOW!!! I'm so glad I called him and requested an in-person meeting. How can you get the true message of something across through an email? Belly to belly is always best.

I had been gone for about a week and when I came back I noticed that not only were there two benches installed at the hospital's Heart Center entrance, but two more benches had also been placed at the main entrance. Cool!

Then benches began to pop up all over the hospital grounds. In total, I think there were over ten benches set up for our patients, visitors and team members to sit on. I later found out that the hospital used to have benches a long time ago, but they took them down because homeless people were sleeping on them. Well, that's another opportunity to be a Catalyst for Change!

I heard so many excuses about why we couldn't get the front walkways cleaned regularly it was ridiculous. We have 7-12 seconds to make a first impression, so we need to be walking in through the front entrance of our practice or hospital or office to see what our patients and other visitors see. But now I noticed the front entrance was SO clean! I made a note to call Plant Operations to share how thankful I was that it looked so good.

It was Catalyst for Change moment when a VP told me, "Merikay, don't sweat the small stuff." Well, I disagreed, we needed to be sweatin' the small stuff if we wanted to be successful. *Where do you need to sweat more of the small stuff in your organization?*

Mr. Plant Ops also helped me get the padding installed in the tube systems throughout the nursing unit hallways. When I saw him on one of the units one day, I asked why there was a hold up on getting these fixed. He said, "Merikay we've been workin' on that since I got here." I said, "Well, how long is that?" He replied, "18 years." I replied, "That's too damn long."

He laughed and then showed me part of the other problem with the tube system. For those of you that may not know what I'm talking about, when some medication are delivered from the pharmacy, for example, they can be sent through a tube system from floor to floor. Kind of like the tubes that you see at the bank teller. Anyway, if tubes accumulate in the tube station, they will hit each other and make an awful racket.

So I took a picture with my cell phone, crafted an OREO email and sent it to all the nurse managers, asking for their help to reduce the noise at the nurses station by encouraging the nurses to pick up the tubes in a timely manner.

I had been accused of having 'fresh eyes' on more than one occasion, by more than one senior leader. Since I wasn't afraid to be a Catalyst for Change, some things got changed. Some things didn't. My point is that when it takes forever to see change happen, that's a de-motivator.

Story after story immerged from people who said they had great ideas and no one ever responded to them. Or, if they submitted a TIP – another computerized email opportunity to share an idea for change, they would get a certificate with a few higher up's signatures and a light bulb-shaped stress ball, with a message saying, "Thanks for the Tip". The point is, people will stop sharing ideas after a while if they see no action.

Our final patient experience kickoff was scheduled at the Education Center at LCH on a Sunday at 2 p.m. About 125 employees were supposed to be there. I was the first one to arrive at 12:45 p.m. and I found the room had not been set up. There were full trash cans in every corner, several dirty tables and ones that needed to be dismantled. I noticed the carpet was dirty in several areas too.

Now, on multiple previous occasions I had arrived to meetings where the rooms were not set up properly or were not set up at all. This is both a communication and a process breakdown that kept happening over and over again. In my opinion, nobody was doing anything about it. REALLY????

I made a phone call and a team of Environmental Services people showed up to set up the room, plus a few of the presenters had arrived and began helping. I was using every Dale Carnegie principle I knew not to be upset because I didn't think this should have happened. Presenters needed to be setting up the computer, organizing door prizes and giveaways, and distributing note pads and pens, not emptying trash cans. I don't mind being a team player at all, but this had happened over, and over and over again. LOTS of opportunities for Catalysts for Change if people would only sweat the small stuff.

One of my final suggestions to the Environmental Services team was to set the tables up so the metal bar was opposite where the chair would be. You see, you have to bend over to see the location of the metal bar and understand that if you put a chair on that side, people's knees and legs would be hitting the metal bar. Yes, I sweat the small stuff.

One of the other areas I wanted to change was the chairs in the lobby by the executive offices. They were so low to the floor it was difficult for our elderly patients to stand up from them. I thought to myself one day, "How many people have walked by these chairs and not noticed that?"

I have not always been super comfortable walking up to strangers. I have made myself practice that. When I worked with Arbonne I would talk to strangers at Starbucks, complimenting them on their pocket book or something else in order to strike up a conversation. Nothing happens unless you take a first step.

The key is you have to be genuine and sincere. I have never been a big fan of fake people. If you are nice one minute and back stabbing the next, you go on the broomstick list. I might pray for you, but I might avoid you, too. I found this particularly hard in a big organization. You would have this deep conversation with someone and then a few days later find out they shared something you said in private. You knew from their body language something was different. One coworker accused me of not telling her I was going to be out of the office, so I searched and searched my emails to make sure I had sent her notification. Thankfully I had. So there were only two options: She lied or she was losing her memory.

I am not perfect by any means. I make mistakes every day. My biggest mistake at the hospital was talking to people who I thought were my friends but who turned out to be what I referred to in high school as two-faced. Maybe I was too naïve. Maybe I was too open with people. Either way, my year on the inside was worth it. We got Several benches and padded tube stations. WWHHOOHHOO!!

My proudest accomplishment during my year on the inside was all the graduates from the professional development program that I created to help people improve their ability to set and achieve goals, elevate communications, deal more effectively with stress, improve team performance and impact patient experience. Towards the end of my year on the inside, I received this note from one of our nurse managers:

Merikay,
Thank you for giving so freely of your time and talent to help our group be a stronger team.
I enjoy you so much and you are an inspiration – we're very fortunate to have your input. You have a way of making everything come into focus.

From the heart...

D

I called her to thank her for her inspiring card. It meant so much to me that someone would invest the time to handwrite a note of gratitude. *Who do you need to write a note to today to share how they have impacted you in a meaningful way?*

One of the assignments in the first session of the professional development program was to create a personal mission statement. One of the Emergency Room nurses described her mission this way:

"Life is a gift to be treasured. I will rise each day with thanksgiving on my breath and with the realization that I am far more blessed than some will ever know. I will treat every person I come in contact with as if they are the most important part of my life at that particular moment. I will squeeze every bit of life and experience from every minute in each day, will never take a second for granted, and will learn at every opportunity. When I rest at night I will quiet my mind with the realization that I have given my best and been at my best."

I was so inspired as each session kicked off and people were setting meaningful goals and achieving them. It only took planting seeds of greatness in their hearts and minds. Hearing their accomplishments each session was inspiring. I started keeping copies of testimonials that people would send me during and after the sessions and put them in a "Me" folder on my desktop. As the days got more challenging toward the end of my year on the inside, I wanted to focus on the good stuff more than the bad stuff. *What do you spend your time focusing on? The good stuff or the bad stuff?*

Create your own "I am" statement of what you want to focus on each day, how you want to communicate, lead and serve others. What do your relationships look like? How are you leading yourself and others? What is your attitude and how will you shift to be positive, purposeful and passionate?

_____

_____

_____

_____

_____

_____

_____

_____

_____

_____

_____

_____

_____

_____

_____

_____

_____

_____

_____

The key to making this "I am" statement come alive is to make sure what you write down is what you truly believe. If not, then you are just writing words on a piece of paper. That's why having a True

Mission and Vision is important.

The mission at LRH was honorable, yet people didn't follow it daily. There seemed to be little accountability for people that were not living up the mission statement. From my seat on the bus, after reading the same negative comments over and over, month after month on the patient comment report, I wondered if anyone else was reading these, too? Was anyone doing anything about the targeted areas to improve? Was anyone sweating the small stuff?

The theme of the final LDI that I presented for was "Intentional Leadership." We had a few visitors in the audience from the new health system with which we had recently merged. I read some of the negative comments from the patient comments report to the entire audience. I said, "If we are not reading these comments and doing something about them, we should be ashamed. We need to acknowledge the perception our patients have of their care and explore ways to make it better." Here's the deal, when you are striving to improve, there's no need to focus on the areas in which you already excel. We need to look at the areas where we aren't as strong.

I also showed a video from the Cleveland Clinic about the value of team members impacting patient care through empathy and understanding. https://www.youtube.com/watch?v=cDDWvj_q-o8 I asked two of the hospital's VPs if I could show this video at one of our monthly hospital leadership meetings but, mysteriously, I had been taken off the schedule to speak. They had included a patient experience segment on the agenda, but the CNO and others were presenting, not me.

That was another low moment during my year on the inside. I wished the VPs would have just been up front and said, "Merikay, thanks so much for your contributions, but we've decided to shift this segment at our monthly meetings and offer other people an opportunity to present." Instead, no communication. It made me feel tossed to the side. I chose not to say anything, but inside it hurt.

Speaking is what I love to do. Maybe after my call to action for leaders to take action regarding our patient feedback, they decided I shouldn't get the platform anymore. Or at least a few people made decisions towards the end that directly impacted me and my ability to be a Catalyst for Change. More on that in chapter nine. *How do you handle your low moments? Are you letting them weigh you down or are you using them as learning lessons for the future?*

Two of the professional development sessions focused on human relation principles, with the goal of applying these principles with people at work and at home. How could people use these principles to relate to their patient, family or team member differently? During the class, one manager shared she had applied a few key principles with another manager in her area. Now, after nine years of conflict, they were having lunch together, strategizing on ways to improve their department and even attending a conference together! WOW! She was a Catalyst for Change.

One area where people get into trouble is when they want other people to change. The key is that we have to change ourselves first. That's what happened to me when I used to coach soccer. I was devastated one year when half our team defected to the 'winning' team. I had been the first grade Sunday school teacher of most of the girls that left. The parents didn't tell me that they were not registering their children for our team the following season. That kind of hit me wrong at the time, I wondered why they just wouldn't say, "Merikay, thanks so much for coaching the team the past three years. A group of the kids decided to join a different team this season. Just wanted you to know." I probably still would have been upset about it, but at least I would have known about it ahead of time. Instead I found out about it when the rosters were distributed.

This season I made a commitment to only focus on the positive, to ensure the kids had fun at every practice, to make sure we were focusing on fundamentals and to ensure they laughed and played at every practice. I think that is probably one reason why we had a big defection: I was too serious at times because of my competitive soccer background. After all, the girls were only ten years old and it was a recreation league.

It was the final game of the season and we were playing the team that always won and to which part of my original team defected. We scored first, which was utterly amazing! I bit down hard on a lollipop – yes, I had to bring lollipops, one for each half so I would keep my mouth shut and not say anything - OH what a challenge! Then right before the half the other team scored to tie it up.

At halftime I asked the girls, "Are you having fun? Are you playing hard? Are you doing your best?" That's all I could expect. Right before we said our cheer these were the words of encouragement and coaching I would say to the girls. Have Fun. Play Hard. Do Your Best. You might be thinking "did you win the game?" Yes, 2-1!

The same thing needs to happen in our work life. We need to find ways to have fun (i.e., dress up as a patient and ride in a wheelchair around your campus), we need to play hard and give our best every day.

A huge new sign with LHR's new logo and corporate name was being delivered on campus on a trailer bed hooked on the back of a big truck. I had been walking across the street to my office when a few people began to congregate by the sign. I said, "OH!!! Please take my picture in front of the sign!" I was so excited I began dancing in front of the sign. One employee said, "I want to work with you!" He had no idea how good that made me feel that day.

An hour later emails started going out that said under no circumstances were people supposed to post pictures on Facebook or announce that the new sign was here. WHAT??? First of all, I didn't even know how to post pictures on Facebook and deep down, I thought what a way to kill people's excitement! Of course, I had already emailed the picture to a few of my hospital colleagues because I thought they would find it funny that I was dancing in front of the sign. Apparently there was supposed to be some big sign unveiling with the media involved. Whatever. Somehow some of our leaders managed to take an awesome moment and turn it into a reprimand once again. You get the picture of the culture at LRH? *What is the leadership culture in your organization? Encouraging or critical?*

My biggest goal that wasn't on my performance card determined by my VP or the Planning Department was to be a catalyst for changing the culture. I made it my personal mission to spread happiness, enthusiasm, love, dedication, commitment and kindness. When I asked one of the nurses for her permission to share her mission statement, this was her response:

"Hello!!! How are you doing????? I totally miss your smiling face around our hospital. You were such an inspiration to me and so many others. Of course, you may use my mission statement!! Please keep in touch and keep us posted on all of your fabulous ventures."

Every day you have a choice on what to focus on, who to help, how you want to communicate, who you want to encourage, how you want to lead yourself and others. *How will you inspire or encourage someone today?*

Action Item

Identify someone on your team that needs to be encouraged. Schedule some one-on-one time with them to explore ways you may be able to give them help, inspiration or support.

1 Corinthians 12:7

A spiritual gift is given to each of us so we can help each other.

7 A KISS ON THE HAND

Go out into the world today and love the people you meet.
Let your presence light new light in the hearts of people.
-Mother Teresa

Every month I send a tip out to my database featuring ways we can be Catalysts for Change. The tip may feature a client, a song, book or a video. I want people to find value and application while taking less than three minutes to read it. If you are interested in receiving free monthly tips on creating catalysts for change, visit www.coachmkay.com to register.

Time is precious. It's the one thing we all have in common and the one thing we don't get back. It's interesting when people say, "I just don't have time." I've said that before, haven't you? Well, it's not that we don't <u>have</u> time but that we are not <u>making</u> time. Each of us have 24 hours in a day, so what we do with it is up to us. Yes, there will be mandatory this or mandatory that, yet we do have some control over elements of our day. That's why it's important that we run our schedule and not let our schedule run us. It's important to give yourself time to 'just be.'

I learned this lesson on my first mission trip to Toluca, Mexico. I was walking and talking to our trip leader who had been on three different mission trips with my dad. I told him how I couldn't figure out one of the ladies that was with us. She just didn't seem to be happy about anything and I didn't know what to do to help her. I didn't want to get frustrated or discouraged, yet I found her negativity to be toxic. I thought "We are on a mission trip! This is about helping people and growing in your faith, not about complaining about every little thing!" So I found myself avoiding this women and partnering with other people so I didn't have to listen to her moan and groan. That's when the trip leader turned to me and said, "Merikay, on this trip.... just be."

What wisdom he gave me. You see, he saw I was getting all worked up for nothing. So later that day I found a soccer ball and started teaching the kids who were hanging out at the church how to play soccer. I left the paint brush behind and ran, laughed, played – it was glorious. I completely forgot Ms. Eeyore and decided to have fun. *What do you need to do today to have more fun in life?*

One of the biggest tests of my positivity on this trip happened on the third day. You see there were five women on the trip. One was a pastor and she had her own room with an air mattress on the floor. Note to self and readers: ALWAYS take your own air mattress on a mission trip to avoid sleeping in a room or bed with someone that snores. AND there is a secret to putting ear plugs in correctly. I didn't have any on this first trip – BIG mistake. So after laying awake two nights in a row because of my snoring roommates, I decided to make a pallet out in the hallway.

There was no heat in this house and the marble floor was cold, but I thought well, at least I can sleep and it's quiet. After listening to their four yip, yip dogs, as I like to refer to these furry little creatures that are about as big as a squirrel, I fell asleep.

The next morning, I knew I would probably be cold but I didn't realize I would wake up wet, too! It seems the little yip yip dogs wanted to mark their territory and send a clear message to me I was laying in their space! Yep, they peed all over my bedding – with me in it! This was my affirmation that morning: "This trip is for the Lord, this trip is for the Lord, this trip is for the Lord."

I had to find some humor in it! Some of the best things we can do in life are to find humor, discover the blessings, and look for joy first. During my year on the inside, this was one of my challenges at LRH. So many of the people in leadership always looked at the negative first in every situation. I was used to looking at all the ways things would work or seeing the best in people or giving people the benefit of the doubt. Some of the leaders with whom I spent most of my time always found the worst in people, looked at all the negative sides of situations and always brought up reasons why things hadn't worked or wouldn't work.

So I had another secret goal: to get these people to put their sunny glasses on and see the world through a different lens. I realized this is just how they were wired, so instead of letting it get me depressed, I chose to use it as lighter fluid. Well, what if we did this? What if we tried again? What if it were different?

There were a few strides made, but ultimately I had to let go. I realized for me to continue to be a Catalyst for Change, I needed to get out from under the umbrella of limited thinking. I was a big picture, dreamer, activator personality; being trapped in a box was no place for me. *Where do you need to change your thinking to be a Catalyst for Change?*

One day I stopped by the Emergency Department to round on the waiting area. One of the nursing assistants approached me with a piece of paper. On it was a patient's name, two phone numbers, her room number and the words "eye glasses". So the hunt began. First, I found the security officer so he could let me in the lost and found closet, then traveled to the fourth floor to get a description of the glasses directly from the patient, then back down to the ED. It was then that I noticed a man in his mid 40's, sitting on the edge of a bed in the hallway. legs dangling over the edge and swinging. When he looked at me, I smiled, nodded and said "hi", but I kept walking. I was on a mission to find eye glasses.

On my next walk through in the ED a few minutes later, our eyes met again. This time I stopped and said, "Do you need a blanket?" He pointed to the one folded on the bed beside him and said, "No, I got one, thanks."

"Are we taking good care of you?", I asked. He said, "Yes, I'm here to detox, gotta get off the alcohol." "Good for you," I said, "strong people are the ones that seek help. You are in the right place and I'm so glad you are here."

"My boss wants me to get healthy," the patient continued. "I need to keep my job." "That's awesome you have his support," I replied. "In three weeks we get another big order to make furniture and I gotta be there," he said.

As a former adjunct chaplain at Wesley Long Hospital, I felt comfortable asking the patient, "Can I say a prayer for you, that's kinda how I roll?" He replied, "That would be great." "How 'bout right now?," I asked, and I put my hand on his shoulder. We bowed our heads and I lifted him up, asking for continued strength, more courage, and excellent caregivers to surround him. I reinforced how proud he should be that he came to the hospital for help. We said a word of thanks and AMEN. That's when he grabbed my hand and gently kissed it and said "Thank you." I held back tears, smiled real big and said, "You're welcome."

As I walked away, I couldn't help but wonder how many people walked by this man as he sat on the gurney with his feet dangling over the side. *Who have you walked by today? If you could have a 'do over' what would you do differently?*

Next time you are walking down the hallway in your organization and you see a complete stranger, or a customer or an employee, stop and ask them how they are doing. Ask them if they are receiving good services or care. Ask them how they are being treated or what they love about their job or if there are concerns that need to be addressed. You never know what you may discover.

I haven't always been comfortable praying with people. Three years serving as an adjunct chaplain helped grow my comfort level. I joined my first bible study at my church several years ago, which also helped. Praying out loud with a small group of women helped build my confidence. Whenever our study leader asked for someone in the group to open or close with a prayer, if no one raised their hand, I would volunteer.

Researchers say the number one fear is public speaking. Looks like we can add praying out loud to that list, too, because I have served on several committees at church and find it amazing how many people on those committees are afraid of praying out loud. Since we aren't born with the fear of public speaking, it looks like we learn to develop that over time.

My hope is that more people will take a risk and build this as a skill set because I think we need more prayer in more places with more people. Amen! *What fear do you need to overcome to become a Catalyst for Change to improve your career, relationships or life?*

Each time I walked across campus to the main hospital, I would always try to enter a different way. This gave me the opportunity to see different people, check out the doorways and stairwells for cleanliness, look for trash on campus, check for parking congestion, dance in front of new signs, etc. I was always checking things out and trying to observe my surroundings. An event that happened within the first few months of my arrival at LCH taught me the importance of being aware of your surroundings.

I was in a meeting in the 505 Building, near the main hospital. A walkway connects the building to the lower level of the hospital. An exterior stairwell led up one level to the entrance of the administrative offices and hospital's heart center. This is where I always ran into Mr. Parking RN. As I'm hurrying back to the administrative offices for a meeting with my VP, I noticed a woman hunched over and holding her side.

As I came closer, we made eye contact and I said, "Hello." I kept walking quickly because I was going to be late for my meeting. Suddenly the woman stopped walking and said, "Do you know where outpatient radiology is?" I replied, "Umm, I think it's in that building, as I pointed to the 505 Building but continued walking.

After a few steps, I turned around and ran back to the lady and said, "You know what? I'm not 100% sure it's in that building, so I'm gonna go with you to make sure." As we walked together, she said, "I'm late and I don't want to miss my appointment." She was huffing and puffing and holding her side, yet her gait was pretty fast for someone that looked like she might be in pain.

We arrived in the lower level of the 505 Building and she began breathing really heavy and was turning pale. I looked around quickly for some hospital employees, especially someone who looked clinical. Fortunately there were some employees who had their badges pinned to the upper right of their clothing, so I could find some help quickly. "Can you please get a wheelchair for me?", I asked.

At this point the lady was hunched over the water fountain, trying to catch her breath. I was prepared for the worst, yet didn't want that to go down at this particular moment. I have watched nearly every episode of ER and Grey's Anatomy, so I knew what potentially could transpire.

She then disclosed to me, "I have COPD and have trouble breathing sometimes." I was thinking "Oh crap! This is one of those moments my sister the RN warned me about." I said, "Just relax, breathe slowly, and we will get you to your appointment."

Moments later the wheelchair arrived and I confirmed with the employee exactly where we were supposed to be. We were in the wrong place and needed to head over to the main campus near the administrative offices where I was headed in the first place. So I looked at her, asked her name, and said, "Why don't you have a seat and I'll wheel you over there." She said, "I'll be fine, I can make it."

I was thinking, "Hell no, you're not fine." Instead I chose to say, "Look, I'm the mom of three kids, so don't make me turn into mommy mode! You need to get in this chair and I'm happy to wheel you over to the other building." I turned into my sister right before my eyes.

My sister is a little bossy. She still bosses me around even though she is almost a foot shorter than I am (something I love to remind her about when we stand next to each other). Now she is older by one year, one month and one day, so that gives her the right as sibling to still boss me around, no matter how old we each get year by year. This personality trait has served her well when she is dealing with difficult patients, or as I like to refer to them, terminally unique people. You know the type. No matter what, they will find the most difficult or challenging route, making it difficult or challenging for themselves and all the people around them. All of this in spite of the fact that you have used every single human relations or customer service principles you have ever learned trying to help them!

I learned several lessons in this experience. First, be aware of your surroundings. You never know when someone you pass by will need your help. If I hadn't made eye contact with this patient and said hello, she might not have felt comfortable asking for help. Also, when I chose to continue walking without really knowing for sure if I was recommending the correct location, I wasn't following one of our standards of behavior: escort to destination. Lastly, sometimes you have to be assertive with people. If I had given in when this patient said she didn't need a wheelchair, she may not have arrived safely to outpatient radiology.

When we arrived at the outpatient office I went in with the patient and rang the bell. I hated that we had to ring a bell. I wished there would always be someone there to greet us in person. The other thing I hated is that soap operas or news was generally playing on the TV above the registration desk – yuck! You know how I feel about news and soap operas? Really? Another Catalyst for Change moment was a phone call to the co-director of that department who was receptive to the idea of changing that station to The Care Network, which showcased beautiful scenery and soft easy listening music.

Thanks to our service team and the stick-to-it-ness of one of the VPs, the Care Network had been installed on televisions throughout in the hospital. But one of the challenges was making sure the patients knew about this new offering. It was important that the staff not only knew about it, but that they offered it to the patients.

We also invested in ear plugs and night masks to help ensure patients experienced quietness at night so they could rest better and heal. I never really felt like we maximized the distribution of that inventory. One researcher shared that on average patients lose at least two hours of sleep per night while in the hospital. If you are being woken up for tests or for blood draws or because your mattress is constantly inflating and deflating, or the staff is too loud at the nurses station, that just adds to the sleep deprivation. What good is it to have ear plugs, the Care Network or eye masks if the patients or staff don't know about it and it's not being recommended or used?

Another Catalyst for Change initiative during my year on the inside was signs that featured cute little kids dressed up in lab coats and scrubs, with their index finger up over their mouth and a caption reading, "Shhh. Thank you for keeping the noise down to provide a safe and healing environment for our patients." The signs were awesome except they were too small. We were told they were going to be resized, but I never saw it happen while I was there. Other priorities took precedence. It's unfortunate because the idea was great, but the implementation was poor.

Some service team members weren't sure the signs were hung in exactly the right places. In retrospect, we should have asked several family members where they thought we should place the signs. We placed them on each patient care floor by the elevator doors, near a small sign that showed room numbers. Some of the service team members thought they should have been placed higher up on the wall, more eye level near the larger signs on the hallways that showed the room numbers.

When I visited my father when he was a patient at Duke University Hospital, I didn't spin around when I got off the elevator to look for room numbers. I would look down the hallway for the signs to room numbers. So the location of these signs at LHS didn't make sense to me, either. You would only see them as you were standing waiting for the elevator. I mentioned it a couple of times to the VP responsible for the signage. Things need to be a priority to people or they won't get done.

When the members of the patient experience department from

the merging hospital visited with us for the day, we were so excited to walk them around the hospital, introduce them to people, share the things we were focusing on and learn the cool things they were doing to improve the patient and family experience. We were a department of two with an intern serving a population of 2,200 staff and, on average, 170-220 patients per day.

As we walked them down to the cafeteria, I stopped in the hallway and said, "This is one thing we are working on getting changed." The old standards of behavior from several years before was posted, the old rewards and recognition program was highlighted and the old mission and vision of the organization was posted. I had started working on updating these, along with developing a decent campus map, with our marketing department during my first few months on board. Again, it seemed like I was sweating the small stuff to some people, but why would you have information posted that had been out of date for over a year? Some information was two or three years old. The reason may have been because people just didn't care or think it was important or because of budget constraints. I got so tired of waiting for the old stuff to come down, I asked a plant operations team member if he would help me peel the stuff off the board. It was just a thin laminate poster that had sticky stuff on the back. He said, "No problem, Merikay. I can get this down."

Why did it take months for the marketing department to update it? Well, they had a plan, we just didn't know about it. It seemed that they were going to order acrylic holders so the posters could be interchanged. Great idea. When they went up, they looked great! Except one was mounted crooked. I didn't say anything because I was just sweating the small stuff.

Maybe my quest for excellence came from dentistry. What if the veneers are crooked when they are placed on your front teeth? What if the color of the crown was two shades lighter or darker than it should have been? What if my father made an incision over the tooth for a flap procedure and cut too much tissue away on the gum line? In business today, if we want to be competitive, if we want to separate ourselves from the pack, we need to sweat the small stuff.

I also noticed in the entrance way in the emergency department that there were photos of physicians who no longer worked at the hospital. As you have probably already noted, there were plenty of opportunities to sweat the small stuff!

It's interesting to me how complicated things can become in a large organization. I came from a world where you identify a problem, find a solution, involve key people, move on the solution and celebrate success. In this culture, if you moved ahead on things without involving the right people or asking for permission, you were scolded. Catalyst for Change moment. If I didn't have thirty human relation principles in my back pocket at all times to interface with all the different personalities, plus an awesome resource in the book, Dealing with People You Can't Stand, I would have never survived as long as I did.

I kept hoping with every conversation, with every email, with every meeting, with every graduating class from the professional development program, with every voicemail, with every coaching session, we would create this small army of change catalysts. And we were beginning to see some positive results. Team members were being kinder to each other, showing more compassion to patients, being more helpful, smiling more. The patient experience sessions help jump start that momentum.

While I was grateful to the hospital leadership for many things, I also got frustrated with leadership for many things. Because I tried my best to focus on the positive, I was grateful that they invested time, money, resources and talent into those three hour sessions to re-boot our culture and recommit our workforce to the patient experience.

I was also grateful to my VP for allowing me to design and deliver the professional development classes to various employees throughout the hospital. Yet I was disappointed that no one from senior leadership participated, despite numerous invitations. Most of them attended at least one final session and one senior leader told me, "If you wanted me to come to a session, you should have sent the date out weeks in advance." Well, not sure if I wanted her energy in the room anyway. *What do people say about you when you leave a room? Some people brighten a room by leaving. Let's make sure it's not you or me.*

One of the blessings about pushing myself to meet so many people and really making an effort to get to know them is that when I needed something or when someone else needed something, I could call or show up in the department and things usually got done pretty quickly. For example, I was rounding one day in the ED and noticed two of the nurses had a concerned look on their faces. I walked up to them and said 'Hey, what's going on? Do you guys need something?" One of the RN's replied, "Yes, we have a lady here who doesn't have any clothes, and no one to bring her any, so we are trying to figure out what to do."

Now, I had brought clothes to donate to large bins that the ED team kept in their supply closet. I would go in there every month or so to organize the clothes, see what kind of stuff was in there and what they may need. I knew we didn't have any women's clothes and the nurse said she needed a size 2 XL. So I responded, "Well, I could run to Walmart or I could try to get her a scrub top and pants." I knew driving Walmart would take too long, especially if the patient was ready to be discharged, so I said, "Let me go to the surgery department and see what I can do."

As I got ready to go upstairs, I thought it may be quicker to see if the laundry and linen department could provide scrubs. I went downstairs, rang their buzzer. One of the ladies who had been in my teambuilding session months before answered the door: "Hi, what can I do for you?" I told her the patient's story and she took me to the laundry/linen manager and he hooked me up with clean scrubs. Beautiful! And it only took about three minutes for me to leave the ED, retrieve scrubs and head back to the ED to assist this patient in need. This is where rounding can be so beneficial – you never know who you can help.

The house supervisor looked at me one day and said, "Merikay, I've seen you more in the past year that I've seen administration in ten." Once again it made me feel good that she acknowledged my visibility yet sad that our leadership wasn't more visible. Leaders need to be with their people. They don't need to hover, but they need to be present on a daily basis. One president of a hospital system told me he spends 35% of his time rounding. When he said that to me I told him I wanted to lean over the table and kiss him. He just smiled and chuckled. I know there are meetings and emails and more meetings and more emails. But somehow leaders need to figure out how to be with their people. *How much time do you spend rounding in different departments in your organization? If you are a business professional, how much time do you spend having daily huddles or monthly team meetings or yearly retreats?*

I had never heard of the term "rounding" until I worked for

LRH. In the restaurant business we did walk-throughs. We would walk through the kitchen to check for cleanliness, walk through the walk-in cooler or freezer to check for first in, first out, walk through the dining area to do random table visits to see how guests were enjoying their meal, walk around the building to see how the grounds looked. So when I found out more about purposeful rounding in the hospital, it made so much sense. I didn't understand why more senior leaders didn't do it more often.

One of the great ways LRH began recognizing improvements in patient satisfaction was by giving high performing departments the Big Cup Award. It was decided that the service team and several hospital leaders (C-Suite and VP's) would meet at 1:30 p.m at the hospital's patient entrance, then take the Big Cup trophy to the department receiving the recognition. The idea came from a hospital best practice which had been presented at a Press Ganey conference which several of us had attended in Maryland in 2012. To earn this honor, the department had to have high patient satisfaction survey results and had to be able to indicate what specific steps they had taken to garner such results. The Big Cup trophy traveled from department to department, with the previous winning department decorating the cup before presenting it to the newest recipient.

How does your organization recognize and reward people? Do you have a budget for R&R (not rest and relaxation, but recognition and rewards) and do you honor people in a timely basis?

We wanted to recognize the nurses in the Emergency Department because their scores had improved greatly over a six month period. Since we had conducted a brief questionnaire during one of their monthly staff meetings, we knew the majority of respondents said they wanted to be recognized with food (chocolate was a big hit, too). So I thought we would just set a date, call food services or a catering company and, whambam, make it happen! Instead it took over two months for ED nursing leadership to plan and execute the event. By that time we had lost a lot of our momentum.

R&R needs to be conducted in a timely manner. What message does it send when it takes extended periods of time to recognize or reward your employees? What if Olympians had to wait eight weeks to receive their medal? What if the winner of the Super Bowl had to wait until summer to receive their trophy? Get the picture? As leaders we need to get on it and get to it quickly!

What do you do if you have no funds for R&R? One of the creative ways our hospital funded the R&R program was using the profits from the drink and snack machine sales. I thought that was brilliant!

Peer-to-peer recognition is important, too. LRH created a simple form on half-sheets of paper for employees to recognize one another's contribution to the patient or team experience. These forms were given directly to the team member being recognized or were given to the supervisor or manager to share during one of the department's "starting line-ups" (similar to morning huddles in a dental practice).

Throughout the hospital were small acrylic holders that displayed postcard-sized cards for patients and family members to note excellent care provided by a team member. Here is an example of one of the cards that was sent to our office:

Employee name: Nurses and CNAs
Employee's Department: Fourth Floor
Date: 11/25/13

"The nurses and CNAs on this floor are the most caring and efficient staff I have ever come in contact with. Works cannot express my gratitude from me and my family. Thank you from the bottom of my heart."

When these cards were returned to the patient experience department, we would write a hand written note to those recognized and then forward the card to the manager to review. Then the card was forwarded to the department director and then on to the VP of that department.

Coupons were created for R&R team members, managers, directors, and senior leaders to be used to easily reward team members for providing outstanding service. The team member could take the coupon to the hospital's soda shop or cafeteria to redeem for a cup of coffee, candy bar, bottle water or piece of fruit. A nice gesture for sure!

In order to make it easy to reward team members in a way that would be meaningful to them, the hospital also created a web portal where each employee was asked to share what their favorite snack / drink / color / book / hobby was. Then if people wanted to send a note or purchase something small for an individual, it was simple to find their recognition profile.

The Five Languages of Appreciation, according to author Gary Chapman, are words of affirmation, quality time, acts of service, tangible gifts and physical touch.[11] I hate to admit this, but when my VP cancelled lunch with me last year to celebrate my birthday, initially it was no big deal. Things come up for sure. The problem was she never contacted me to reschedule. I let it hurt my feelings. I know I should have been a big girl about it, but I felt let down. I'm the one that reached out to her to reschedule. Sometimes it's the little things that make a big impact.

Each month at the hospital's director and manager meeting, the names of those who have birthdays that month are called out and people share a round of applause for each person. In my birthday month my name was left off the list. Since I'm not shy when it comes to stuff like this, I said with a big smile, "Hey! I wasn't on the list." The president looked at me and said, "It's not my fault, I didn't make the list." Get the culture point again? There are so many other responses that would have been better. This leader was known for his sarcasm, but I used that response as a Catalyst for Change moment. Leadership is powerful. Strong leadership is inspiring. Poor leadership is demotivating.

There were so many people in the community that respected our hospital president, yet people internally didn't seem that inspired by him. It was frustrating and concerning to hear that people wouldn't listen to his Friday morning messages. Comments such as, "Why should we smile and acknowledge people in the hallways when our own president doesn't?"

Well, one good thing about the patient experience kickoff sessions was they provided an opportunity for EVERYONE to reboot. The president shined at the kickoff sessions by sharing a personal story about how the airline industry made several accommodations to help him fly to be with his family after the death of one of his parents. Most employees had not seen this personal side of him before, and it was refreshing.

Several weeks after the patient experience kickoff sessions, the president told me how much he enjoyed walking through the hallways and greeting people, and how easy it was to do. Sometimes people need to be reminded of the little things that can make a big difference, no matter what your title or position in the organization. It's courteous to make eye contact with people and say "Hello" when you pass them.

I took a few risks on occasion by leaving the president a voicemail or sending an email thanking him for his encouragement or inspiring words and reinforcing how important it was that we send the right messages to people in the organization. When the announcement finally came about the future merger, at one of the director/manager meetings he said something like, "Well, I usually would make some sarcastic remark, but I think this is one of the best decisions for the future of our hospital." Never underestimate the power of words. Words can be encouraging like a fresh flower or harsh like a heavy blow.

At one of the very first director/manager meetings I attended I began a round of applause for the executives as they took the podium. One of the guys seated next to me said, "Oh, no, you're gonna start a new trend." Giving others applause as they take the stage, no matter how small the venue or audience can be encouraging and show appreciation. Since public speaking is the number one learned fear among people, why not give them a few claps and cheers?

Leaders, people will follow your lead. *What kind of leader are you? Are you the kind of leader that recognizes and rewards your team members? Do you use sarcasm as your main form of communication or do you communicate in a way that makes people feel appreciated and important.*

Action Item

Ask your team members how they would like to be recognized and rewarded. Explore ways you can enhance your R&R program.

Deuteronomy 15:10

Give freely without begrudging it and the LORD your God will bless you in everything you do.

8 MY 'AHA' MOMENT

*The ultimate measure of a man is not where he stands in moments
of comfort and convenience, but where he stands at times
of challenge and controversy.*
-Martin Luther King Jr.

Have you ever had that moment when you thought, "Aha! I get it!"? Maybe it was a conversation with someone and he/she said something that set off a spark of insight. Maybe it was observing how someone at work handled a certain situation. Maybe it was a speaker or professor who made a point and you connected with it in some way. Maybe it was a risk you took professionally and it yielded awesome results. Maybe it was a comment or thought that you made that took you to the dark side and you realized you needed to make a change. This happened to me recently.

I was at a dinner party and one of the couples coming to the dinner had been long time friends of my husband at his former job. The dynamic years ago? They were both married to other people. The dynamic now? They were divorced and dating each other. I was THRILLED about this because I thought each of them was so positive, engaging, interesting and talented. It was wonderful that their lives intersected again and I wanted to share how happy I was for them. I had to catch myself before I said anything, because my first thought was, "Matt, your wife was never very friendly. She seemed so unhappy all the time and I never saw you guys have any fun."

That would have been horrible for me to say and I was surprised that I was even thinking it! My 'aha' moment was that you have to be careful of the people you surround yourself with because it is super easy to fall into the trap of gossip, negative thinking or criticism. You also need to be aware of what you are reading, watching on Netflix or listening to on the radio.

I hate to admit this, but I watched the entire episodes of "House of Cards" and "The Borgias" on Netflix. It is true that you can binge watch these shows and I'm proof they can be addicting. It was my escape during my 12-week sabbatical from stress. Yes, that's right, I stepped off the world. My former neighbor used to say, "Merikay, sometimes you have to give yourself permission to step off the world, and when you are ready, jump back on."

In fact, just this morning I shared with my coach, business partner and friend that I was feeling centered and excited about the new business focus of COACH MKay Companies. As she was sharing where she was in life – recovering from rotator cuff surgery, finishing up coursework from graduate school, going to rehab several times per week, and enjoying spring weather, she said, "You have to be very disciplined. I have a new lifestyle now. I want to be around for a long time and dance again and throw a Frisbee. It has become my priority to heal. Life happens. Sometimes I have to stop. Now I know what I want to do and what I don't want to do."

I took notes as she was sharing. This was so insightful to me. I felt connected to her words and had many 'aha' moments. I shared with my friend that I had written notes during our conversation and I told her about all the new business opportunities that had been presented to me over the past few weeks. I said, "It was so interesting to me because once I got clear on my methodology, the types of people I wanted to work with, the types of projects I wanted to spend my time on and the people that I thought would be valuable to partner with – things are starting to happen."

If we aren't careful our life, business and relationships can get off track and we may not even know it. The church that I have been a member of for over 40 years is going through BIG changes. One of the pastors who has been with our congregation for close to fifteen years is moving out of state with his family. The other pastor who has been with our church for nearly twenty years is battling cancer. We also have a new senior pastor entering his second year.

An email went out to 8-10 people asking for help as liturgist over the summer for one of the four services. I knew that in order for me to assist our church in this way, I needed to be strong mentally, emotionally, spiritually and physically. I needed to get my mind right and focus on the right stuff.

So I'm getting on track with devotion time, watching White Collar on Netflix for my down time (much easier on the mindset), reading inspirational business books again, avoiding negative people and situations, playing tennis and golf, spending quality time with my family, going on date nights with my husband. All these things take effort. If you don't make the time to understand what you want to do differently, make a plan to actually do things differently, and execute your plan efficiently, then it's difficult to be a Catalyst for Change in your life or in your business. Life Happens. *Where have you had an "aha" moment lately? How will you use it to identify opportunities for positive change?*

So what happens if you are in a job where the majority of the people you work with seem unhappy, and morale, engagement and performance are low? You have three choices: either don't let it impact you or be a Catalyst for change or leave. It's difficult if you are unable to insulate yourself emotionally, physically, mentally from this type of negative environment.

One of the blessings at LRH was the pockets of excellence that kept me on fire -- select groups of people at all levels in the organization that would whisper change to me in the hallways or during meetings or on a phone call. One surgeon that had been with the organization for multiple years shared with me his passion for one of his hobbies. I noticed so much happiness, contentment, joy and excitement in his eyes. Then when we switched to talking about the hospital and some of the politics of business, his forehead tightened, his smile faded and his tone became more direct. In fact, one of the last things he said to me was, "Be careful Merikay." I think he realized the number of risks I was taking daily to create change in our organization and that if certain people disliked my assertiveness or found out about my ideas or conversations, they may not take too kindly to it.

There are different types of leaders. Some leaders embrace and listen to ideas, some avoid listening at all cost, some leaders listen with the intent to do something, some leaders listen with no intent to do anything, some leaders listen and do the same thing over and over. We all know what doing the same thing over and over again (or a different version of the same thing) and expecting different results is defined as? INSANITY. *Which category do the leaders in your organization fall into?*

There will be people that God places in your path for a reason, for a season or for life. I believe that we have opportunities to learn at every turn if we open our hearts, minds and souls to ideas. Some of the people that come into our life are temporary – we have an opportunity to impact them in some way or maybe they make an impact on our life. There are people that come into our path and may be there forever. FAMILY, yes, we are stuck with them, whether we like it or not.

One of my "aha" moments with my family was when my brother would not return my phone calls or emails. Three or so years had passed since my mother had died and I missed my younger brother. My kids missed him and they had loved hanging out with him. There were moments when I thought, "I'm never calling him again. I'm not calling until he calls me first. I can't believe he hasn't emailed me back." Then I would remember he's my brother, and keep knocking gently, hoping maybe the door would be opened.

I was at the hospital looking over my calendar for the upcoming holidays. We were on mandatory furlough and I was trying to figure out how to take the vacation I had left before the end of the year and also take the required furlough without missing too many meetings or planned work engagements. I wanted to take off a half-day on Wednesday before Thanksgiving to prepare the house because my sister and her husband, two kids were coming over for the holiday. Thankfully, I knew of an awesome local restaurant which served great home cookin', so I brought three of my casserole dishes for the owner of Becky & Mary's (not changin' the name on this one – y'all need to give them a visit) to fill to the brim with sweet potatoes, macaroni and cheese, and potato salad. Yes, I've never had a problem putting other people's home cooked food into my casserole dishes. I don't even mind telling people that I bought it at Harris Teeter or from Becky and Mary's. It's the thought that counts right?

It was two days before Thanksgiving when my cell phone rang. It was my brother. "I'm not mad at mom anymore and I miss my family", he said. I replied, "Well, good. Get your butt over here in two days because we are eating Thanksgiving here at my house and

Allison and her family are joining us." He called me a couple of days post-Turkey Day and left a long message about how much fun he had, how he thought things would have been awkward and they weren't, and how glad he was he came. Knock gently and the door just might swing open. *What relationship do you need to spend some time healing, repairing, forgiving or building?*

One relationship that I was interested in building was with Greg – the president of the entire health system with which our hospital had just merged. I had met him in person several months earlier and the engagement was an AHA moment for sure. You see, my uncle knew his father; they were friends and had spent time on the river together for years.

When I heard that Greg would be at LRH, I called my uncle to confirm it was the same person he had mentioned to me a few years earlier. So when Greg and his leadership team arrived in the lobby, I mentioned my uncle and his face just lit up! Greg was so personable.

A few months later I was visiting family and mentioned to my uncle, who was a retired physician and hospital administrator, of my concerns and findings at the hospital during my year on the inside. He encouraged me to reach out to Greg. It took me several months, but I finally called Greg's administrative secretary and requested a meeting.

There were only a handful of people at LRH that knew I was going to the main health system site to meet with the President. When you feel called to protect the lambs, you answer the call. I sent an agenda to Greg with four talking points and asked for thirty minutes of his time. My proposed agenda included::

1-Learn more about your background and leadership impact
2-Share current challenges and MK's observations
3-Anything else you want to add

Here's the deal. I didn't believe the System really knew what was happening on the inside of our organization. I picked four challenges to discuss that revolved around leadership, patient experience, employee morale and accountability. Our meeting lasted almost an hour and the response was, "Some of these things I suspected, some of them I didn't know. We will turn things around."

I felt peace in my heart on my drive home that Greg would do something. He inspired me that day when he said, "Merikay, I spend 70% of my time on the floor every day with my people." WOW!!!!!!! When he said that, I responded, "I might just lean over the table and kiss you." Okay, so maybe that would have been awkward – but none the less, I was moved.

Greg helped me believe again in the possibility of transformational leadership. I had to believe that this System was going to be the knight in shining armor and make our organization better.

He asked me why I was leaving the organization. I said because of my family. That's what I wanted everyone to think at the hospital. I didn't want people to know that I was leaving because I didn't have faith in our leadership. I was losing my ability to inspire and encourage other people. My posse knew the deal.

When you are at a point in your career that you no longer believe in leadership, it may be time to move on. It is by far my biggest regret, yet I would not have traded that time. I learned so much and met so many wonderful people. It's critical that you look for the bright spots at every turn. It's easy to look on the dark side, to see the worst, to think the worst. You have to push yourself to see the best in people and in the situation.

There are people in your life that will help you realize the type of leader you want to be and the type of leader you don't want to me. My former instructor and manager in Dale Carnegie called me the "moral compass" of the team. I thought it was a compliment originally, and then after several interactions I realized that our business mindset arrived at different intersections. When I put my counseling hat on to evaluate our relationship, I realized she was a survivor, the youngest of several brothers, competitive in nature and wanted to thrive in all areas of her life. She was a top rated instructor and top rated in sales. She was successful.

Me? I was not as successful financially in the business and at times focused too much on helping people. Sometimes my caring meant I gave my time away, didn't fill my pipeline properly, didn't ask the tough questions to close the sale, or dig deep to find out what was blocking us from doing business. I was gullible at times and if someone told me they would do something, I believed them. When I lost over $40,000 in revenue because of not having a signed contract and because the decision maker changed his mind about hosting our retreat, I knew I better become stronger and more of a bulldog if I wanted to be successful in sales. Now I'm a bit more cautious, a bit more strategic, and I ask tougher questions. I still take risks and want to help people; I just make sure it's done in a way in which I don't feel as if I'm getting taken advantage of and that my business doesn't suffer because of my compassion.

One of my last phone calls for my work with Dale Carnegie was with a training director from one of the most prestigious companies in Greensboro, and it was an AHA moment for me in sales. I had been one of the instructors for a presentations program in a class held on-site at the company and I was trying to explore additional business opportunities with them. A participant in our class was trying to help by connecting me to other people in the organization. Instead of keeping the HR contact who had assisted with coordinating the initial sessions out of the loop, I thought I should call her to share the information from the conversation I had had with one of her employees. I didn't want her to feel like I was going behind her back.

WOW! She shut me down quickly and told me to refrain from contacting any employees in the organization; every call was to go through her. I thought it was a power play and realized that maybe she didn't like the fact that I was trying to build relationships with other people in the company. Well, I knew that my manager, being the savvy bulldog that she was, would not be pleased that I had not penetrated the account further. I not only felt like I let down the employees that wanted additional training, but now I felt like I was letting my boss down because the doorway was being shut by this HR training contact. I know you are thinking, "Merikay, you are way too sensitive." Well, you're right, I am at times and if we are going to be successful in business today, we need to keep our emotions in check.

I remember sitting in my car as I was picking up my daughter from soccer camp on that hot summer day thinking how disappointed I was that someone would think I would purposefully do something that would negatively impact them. In a shaky voice I told her, "You don't know me. I'm not comfortable continuing this conversation and I'm hanging up now." That was my "aha" moment: this type of sales was not for me anymore.

Well, here's the good news. All of my experiences have helped me learn a tremendous amount about business, people and sales. I also realize that I prefer to view people and think, "He or she is doing the best they can."

It's easy to focus on all the things that don't work; what's more difficult is focusing on things that do work. I'm a work in progress and still struggle at times with taking things personally. I want to sleep well at night and know that I did my best, helped my best, loved my best, forgave my best, and put it all on the table.

I would be lying if I said that I wasn't disappointed in how things ended at the hospital or for the training company or for the healthcare consulting firm or for the restaurant that I worked for, but without these experiences I would not be the person I am today. I would not be the leader I am today. I would not have continued to pursue owning my own company. I would not have realized the powerful ways to treat people, to lead, to create Catalysts for Change, to forgive, to grow, to be flexible, to stretch, to fail and to succeed.

It's been quite some time since I left the hospital, yet each month I pick a few people from the organization to call and say "Hello!". I finally decided to go back on occasion and have lunch in the hospital cafeteria. I had embraced the possibility that maybe security would escort me off the property but if they did, I would enjoy it because I had conducted a workshop for their department and most all of them knew me and I thought highly of them. I especially liked the security director and two of the guards that had participated in our professional development series, so I secretly hoped it would be one of them.

As I walked into the cafeteria, I made eye contact with one of the cafeteria workers who had made such a positive impact on me while I was there. She will never know how her words of encouragement, her words of praise, her desire for positive change, her ability to see good in others gave me fuel. She winked and left her food station to come and give me a BIG hug.

A nurse said, "Where 'ya been?" I smiled and said I had left at the end of December to work for my company again and it was super to see her. Several other nurses said hello and I replied, "Oh, can we please take a selfie? It's so good to see you all!!!" Of course I had to post it later that day on my Facebook page. Yes, I finally learned how to navigate Facebook, so please visit my FB page @coachmkay.

One nurse stopped by our table and said, "Merikay, I was just telling someone yesterday about your OREO model and we used it to help one of my nurses communicate better with another employee."

I walked over to the area where the environmental services team sits and greeted several people, asking how they were and telling them it was good to see them. Another nurse stopped by the table, I stood up, gave them a BIG hug and said, "I miss you all." She said, we miss your smile and energy!"

I made a promise to several people that day that I would come back monthly to eat in the cafeteria. I only have six days left in this month, so I better schedule it now or I may miss the mark!

Over 20 people stopped by our table or greeted me in the hallway on my first visit back to the place where I had my year on the inside. It was wonderful to see all these hardworking, dedicated people who are committed to being their best, giving their best and providing the best care they possibly can. *How would you rate the people in your organization when it comes to giving their best? Do you know what needs to change to help them give their best? Do you need to change some of the people on your team? Do you need to look at opportunities for professional development? Do you need to take a break and re-evaluate what you are doing with your career?*

I'm amazed at the number of people that do not use all the vacation time awarded to them on an annual basis. The Huffington Post shared an article about this which states "Unfortunately, all too many of us could be on vacation but choose not to. That's the finding of a striking and important new study released this morning by Travel Effect, an initiative of the U.S. Travel Association. Entitled "Overwhelmed America: Why Don't We Use Our Paid Time Off?," the study found that 40 percent of American workers will leave paid vacation days unused." Another unfortunate aspect about vacation is that when people finally take time off, they check their phones the entire time! I admit, I suffer from cell phone attachment at times and have to force myself to put it away. To read the full article, visit: http://www.huffingtonpost.com/arianna-huffington/paid-vacation-days_b_5693225.html

This year my vacation was cut short. It was an "AHA" moment. In sixty short days, I had focused so much on providing care/coordination for my kids during summer break, and coordinating the Swim for Cancer efforts for our local pool, and volunteering for other capacities, that I neglected to spend enough quality time on what I enjoy the most: my business.

So when I exploded during our family vacation, I decided to come home and collect my thoughts. I asked my husband to stay at the beach with our kids because I needed time to figure some things out. I needed a retreat. I do retreats for business all the time, now I needed to do it for my personal well-being. What was going to be my focus, where was my life going, what did I want my future to look like?

Thanks to my new posse – my cousin, a former college roommate, my Coach, my broker – for helping me see some things that I was not seeing clearly. I listened to their recommendations and took some of their advice and had several "AHA" moments. It seems that I had been so caught up in helping/controlling other people and situations, that I had forgotten who I was. Looks like I needed to be a Catalyst for Change for myself.

In two short weeks I found an office outside of my home. I made a few lists to share things more equally, from finances, to chores, to family responsibilities. I didn't realize how much pressure I had let build up in the last several years.

No wonder my vacation wasn't a vacation. I was still cooking, cleaning, organizing (controlling), and helping -- just in a different location with an ocean view! Note to self: when I go on vacation, I'm not cooking and cleaning every day!

My cousin recommended an interesting book called Codependent No More by Melody Beattie. I realized that both my mom and my cousin's mom were codependent. It was up to me to break the cycle.

Here we go! Here's to creating Catalysts for Change! If your business is going great and your personal life is a wreck, that's no good. If your business is horrible and your personal life is great, that's no good. There is a way to find peace in the ups and downs of business and personal relationships. You have to take a time-out sometimes to figure things out.

It was at this time the sad news came about the death of the comedian and actor Robin Williams. Reports stated he suffered from severe depression prior to his suicide. In an interview the television show "Entertainment Tonight", he stated, "I've been married twice and it might have been helpful to learn how to deal with stress. I dealt with it with alcohol."

The outside doesn't always reflect what's happening on the

inside. Losing someone to alcohol and drug addiction is tough. Two words of wisdom: stress kills. It's one of the biggest reasons our hospitals are full today. Stress can be deadly, especially when it turns to worry.

Making healthy choices with exercise, diet, and mindset can reduce stress. I've had seasons where I've made good choices and not so good choices for dealing with stress. *How's your stress level? What "AHA's" have you had from reading this chapter and what changes do you want to make?*

Action Item

Write down all the things creating stress in your life. Review the list and categorize them in one of these four ways: Do, Delegate, Delete, or Pray.

How to conquer worry according to Dale Carnegie:
1. Ask yourself what is the problem.
2. Ask yourself, what are all the possible solutions?
3. Select the best solution.
4. Act.

(From <u>How to Stop Worrying and Start Living by Dale Carnegie</u>)

Matthew 6:27

Who of you by worrying can add a single hour to his life?

9 FOCUS

It's not the load that breaks you down,
it's the way you carry it.
– Lou Holtz

Do you remember a time when you were up all night with a stomach bug spending quality time with the toilet or trash can? I know the thought is somewhat gross. However, this night I was up with my ten year old who caught what we were referring to as the "Beverly Bug." The kids in her carpool and our neighbor, all of whom live on our street – Beverly Place, had the same bug that week, so we knew it was just a matter of time.

Around 8:00 a.m. I texted Lisa in my department to let her know I had been up with my sick daughter most of the night and that I was running late. I asked if she would check my calendar because I couldn't remember if I had any meetings prior to 10:30a.m. I wanted her to contact people if this was the case and let them know I needed to reschedule. She texted back that there were no meetings until 10:30 a.m. Whew! Thank goodness I thought to text her, because not following through on a commitment is difficult for me.

My daughter looked up at me from the sofa with this pale face, and droopy eyes and said, "Momma, you're leaving me?" I replied, "Sweetie, I gotta go to work. I'll call you at lunch and try to be home early this afternoon. I love you and I'm so proud of how strong you are being! Daddy will be here and I'll be back soon."

I got in the car and checked my cell phone: two missed calls from the hospital. At the next stoplight I listened to one of the calls. It was the Senior Director who was my new boss. "Call me as soon as you get this" the message said.

My first instinct prior to working at the hospital would have been to think, "Oh, I hope she's ok," or "I hope everything is alright," or "This must be important." By the tone in her voice I could tell she was upset about something. I was dreading talking to her and knew that I needed to be in a positive frame of mind to teach a leadership class for a group of nurses at 10:30 a.m, so I tried my best to compartmentalize (I know this is not a word, but it's my strategy to put events into compartments and not worry or think about them until you have to). So I turned on the radio to 99.5 because they play continual Christmas tunes during December. Fa-la-la-la-la for the 26 minute drive.

When I arrived, the receptionist on my hall said, "Kelly was here waiting for you for about an hour." I thought that was odd and wondered why she didn't call my cell phone earlier if it was an emergency. I walked down the hall to put my lunch in the fridge and noticed a handwritten note on my doorway that said, "Merikay, call Kelly as soon as you get in." OK, now I'm thinking something is really wrong and either I'm in trouble or someone is hurt.

I called Kelly after I listened to my messages and she said, "I'll be right there." I began to run copies of the communication handout for the session that I was about to teach in 48 minutes, and thought "This could be a nightmare because I need to be positive, focused and on target when I teach." My interactions with Kelly in the past had been all over the spectrum. Sometimes I felt like she was listening, caring and understanding. Other times I felt like she was manipulating, undermining and intimidating. I wasn't sure which Kelly was going to show up at my office.

I saw her coming down the hallway, said, "Hi, what's going on?" We walked into my office and she said, "Merikay, I am waiving the rest of your notice because you have not given me proxy to your calendar. I have asked repeatedly for you to let me know your schedule and I feel you have lost your focus. I need your name badge, Blackberry and your key to the office."

BAM! I said, "OK, so let me get this straight, you are waiving my notice because..." and I repeated back to her what she said. I told her I had texted Lisa that morning to share that I would be late and asked if she needed to see the text. She said, "That's the problem, you don't report to Lisa." Another "aha" moment for me.

Mentally I was thinking this sucks because I'm supposed to teach a class in forty minutes and she is sabotaging that opportunity. Plus I had a meeting scheduled for a group we called the Emergency Department "super friends", a meeting with hospital directors and managers who were teaching a communication program, and shadow segments for one of the nurse managers that I now could not complete. There were now multiple people that I could not say goodbye to in person. All of this was running through my head as Nurse Ratched – oh, I'm sorry, did I just type that? -- as Kelly was sitting in my office.

I circled back mentally to the present, trying to focus. I took off my hospital badge and detached the Christmas Tree wine charm that I had picked up at an ornament exchange party the week before. It looked really cool next to the smiley face sticker that I was scolded for putting on my name badge a few months prior, which I did not remove....purposefully. Holding back tears, I gave Kelly my badge.

OK, so I know deep in my heart that I am willing to stand up for what I believe in and that I have little time or regard for mean spirited people. At this moment though, this nurse was determining my present and that did not make me happy. So I probed a bit further, because I thought certainly there has got to be more to this story...and there was. You see, she said, "One of the nurse managers said you didn't think me or the CNO knew what we were doing. That is so disrespectful." OH, now I got it. This is about control and power. Intimidation and fear.

At this point we were both standing, so I asked Kelly to have a seat. I said, "Kelly, this is what I have a problem with. I don't like the way you treat Lisa. She is a single mom, doing the best she can and you are giving her a hard time about her schedule and wearing a lab coat at work, among other things." Kelly gave me some lame excuse but, frankly, at this point I just wanted her to leave so I could start packing.

I shifted my focus back to the 'leader' in front of me and said, "In fact, we initially were so excited about working in your department but you and Tonia don't include us on anything and don't even know what we do."

I realized I was getting nowhere. I did want to know who else knew about this decision, so of course I asked. She replied, "Me, Tonia and Lynn." So there you have it, the two new 'leaders' and the former 'leader' to whom we reported had decided to waive my notice because I pissed them off and didn't follow their rules. As one of my favorite volunteers told me later that morning, "Merikay, I don't think they realized when they hired you that they had a tiger by the tail."

I told Kelly that I thought she was making a mistake and that I did not agree with her decision. I said, "Well, I'm supposed to teach for Luwanda's group today," and Kelly said she would call her. I said, "They meet in 30 minutes, so I need you to go by the meeting room because they won't know I'm not coming. I would like to know what you are going to say, because the last time I asked you to speak on my behalf, and shared what needed to be said, you said something completely different."

You see, in August I disclosed privately to Kelly that juggling this job and my family had become draining and that I was exploring if the hospital administration would let me work part time. As we sat knee-to-knee after one of the director/manager meetings, I saw someone who listened, cared and understood.

I didn't realize that later she would disclose to Tonia and Lynn my desire. When all four of us met to discuss the realignment of our department, and I asked about the possibility of working part time, Kelly responded, "This is a full time position." I said, "Well, I can't go through another summer like the one I just did, so maybe I'll stay until January or April." Lynn said, "Well, let us know what you decide as soon as possible so we can post the position." There was no "thank you" or "I'm sure this is a tough decision" or "we appreciate all you have done for us" or anything remotely connecting on a personal level. At this point, I really felt like these people didn't give a flip about me as a person. It was a cold meeting and very disappointing.

Back to D-Day. I stood up, thanked her (don't ask me why), extended my hand to shake hers and said, "Well, it's going to take me a couple of hours to pack." She said, "I understand." She walked out and I began to cry. I was disappointed that I couldn't teach that day, couldn't facilitate a meeting, couldn't complete some shadow segments for one of the managers on her floor, couldn't say goodbye to people in person. This was how my year and a half on the inside was going down. Sad for sure.

I picked up the phone and called Lisa, "Well, I've got two hours to clean my office!" She said, "WHAT?" I told her the Cliff note version and said, "Can you help me?" She arrived minutes later. I also called another director, David, who I knew had a truck. We were pretty tight, so when I told him what went down, he said, "I don't know what to say." The ladies on my hallway heard the emotion and I let them know what happened. We openly discussed our celebrations, frustrations and questions. One of the other directors just said, "Merikay, I'm so sorry."

The next several hours were foggy. I just couldn't believe that I was being asked to leave in this way. But the more I thought about it, the more I realized yes, Merikay, this is exactly how they want you to leave…to feel powerless, scolded and defeated. I recalled a conversation earlier in the year with Lynn who said, "Well, if you needle the president enough he might say we don't need a patient experience department." I responded, "Well, that's ok with me." She said, "It's not with me, because you are too valuable." I guess on this day she had decided my worth had declined.

People in leadership positions may be strong, powerful, effective leaders or they may be weak, mean spirited, non-effective leaders. In the end, you have to ask yourself, is the leadership in my organization one that I value, respect, admire? Or is the leadership in my organization one that is disappointing, uninspiring and disconnected? An excellent resource that can help you navigate the waters of connecting to leaders at all levels of an organization is John Maxwell's book, 360 Degree Leadership.

As someone once said, "Life is short and death is far too long." About three months after I left the hospital, I drove to Raleigh to meet with the COO of the health system which had merged with LCH. Why? I had met him briefly at a luncheon a few weeks earlier, and I wanted to get inside his brain, hear his thoughts and perceptions, learn more about his background, and plant seeds for future business opportunities.

I decided to email the president of the entire system to share that I was meeting with his colleague and he responded, "Merikay, I would appreciate it if you would share your candid insight with him." You see, I had taken a HUGE risk a few months earlier to request a meeting with the president of the health system. The good news was I was able to mention the connection of his father with my uncle from West Virginia, so that helped warm up the meeting.

Now only a handful of people from LCH knew I had scheduled this meeting. I felt called to 'protect the lambs' and I knew in my heart our current leadership was not getting things accomplished on multiple levels. At this point I knew my days were numbered and wanted a sense of security that people outside of our organization had a glimpse of what was really happening. Employee engagement was down, employee satisfaction was down, patient experience scores were all over the map, employee morale was down, there was apathy in some of our directors and managers. We had seen a few months after the patient experience kick off sessions when things seemed to be turning around, but nothing stuck.

Have you heard of the Tipping Point? Well, the organization hadn't tipped. LCH slipped back into old ways, old patterns. Leadership wasn't driving with enthusiasm, passion, conviction, positivity, energy, encouragement. We needed more emotion from more leaders to keep everyone fired up!

So why was there apathy? One of the reasons managers and directors were giving up is because they would come up with ideas to save money, create revenue streams, improve employee morale, improve the patient experience, or improve processes and work flow, but senior leaders would not support the initiatives.

Personally, I was losing faith in our senior leaders. I had approached them at different times with ideas and no one would circle back. Or I would be told, "Merikay, I need to do better." And then I would see little to no evidence there was anything different being done. Although I would see a lot of head nodding, I didn't see much action. When I told one senior VP that I needed to take more risks to see positive change, and asked why she didn't take a more active role in creating change for the organization, she said, "I need my job."

I realize I'm not a super patient person, yet when things have been broken for so long in an organization, what do you do? What added to the challenging dynamic in this organization is that many leaders held leadership positions because of years of service, credentials or education achieved, yet with very little leadership ability or leadership training and development. When I mentioned this to Harrison, a senior VP, he looked at me and said, "It's the Peter Principle." I had never heard of it. In case you haven't heard of it, this is how Princeton University describes it:

The **Peter Principle** is the principle that "in a hierarchy every employee tends to rise to their level of incompetence".

This idea was formulated by Dr. Laurence J. Peter and Raymond Hull in their 1969 book, <u>The Peter Principle</u>, a humorous treatise which also introduced the "salutary science of hierarchiology", "inadvertently founded" by Peter. It holds that in a hierarchy, members are promoted so long as they work competently. Sooner or later they are promoted to a position at which they are no longer competent (their "level of incompetence"), and there they remain, being unable to earn further promotions.[21] Peter's Corollary states that "in time, every post tends to be occupied by an employee who is incompetent to carry out their duties" and adds that "work is accomplished by those employees who have not yet reached their level of incompetence". **Managing upward** is the concept of a subordinate finding ways to subtly "manage" superiors in order to limit the damage that they end up doing.

https://www.princeton.edu/~achaney/tmve/wiki100k/docs/Peter_Principle.html

Just because you are a good doctor, nurse, accountant, manager, doesn't automatically make you a good leader. One day the senior HR Director told me a story about when he worked for a construction company early in his career and their best brick layer became a manager. Well, the company lost their best brick layer and then they lost several people on the team because he was a poor manager. Get the picture?

According to T. Falcon Napier of the Institute for Production Tension®, colleges and universities have confused the difference between leadership and management. During an International Management Consulting Meeting, Napier shared the foundations of leadership that were developed in the 1840's and have been adopted by IBM. He's the consultant leading the charge to empower IBM leadership to perform at a higher level. These foundations include:

1. The ability to articulate a compelling vision
2. The ability to awaken and sustain desire in hearts of other people
3. The ability to create and maintain an environment of pride
4. The ability to focus people on a singular destination
5. The ability to identify and develop other leaders[22]

Are you in a leadership position? Count each one of these five foundations as being worth 20 points, and rate yourself on each foundation. Give yourself a score – you know the old grading system, 90-100% = A, 80-90% = B, and so on. How did you do?

There was a vision for our hospital to preserve the culture with our new partner. After the chairman of the hospital board, a respected man in the business community, stated this fact to all the directors and managers during a meeting, I took the podium. "Thank you, Oscar," I said, "for stating that this new partnership would allow us to preserve the culture at LCH. How about we blow up the culture and create a new one?!" What happened next? A round of applause. People were ready for positive change, not same 'ole, same 'ole. The board members only saw things from one perspective, employees of the organization were seeing things from a different perspective.

Okay, enough of the bad stuff, let's focus on the good stuff. There were many positive aspects of the hospital's merger, including access to a talented department dedicated to professional development and leadership training. YEAH!!!

One of the other bright spots came during my meeting with the COO of the system. I had met him a few weeks earlier at a luncheon after my departure from LCH and I wanted to learn more about his background, his leadership experience, and his vision for LCH. I also wanted to share information about my business and to explore potential partnerships for the future. After our discussion he said, "Merikay, the new president will turn things around. I believe in him. It will just take some time." FAITH - it's a powerful five letter word.

Another bright spot was the valuable experience and knowledge I gained by investing 1.5 years working for LCH. There were so many people who inspired me in multiple ways. When I was teaching one of the professional development classes we created to boost performance in goal setting, communications, customer service, leadership and team effectiveness, a participant approached me and said, "Merikay, this class has helped repair a relationship that has been damaged for over 10 years." Another participant said, "Thank you for giving so freely of your time and talent to help our group be a stronger team. I enjoy you so much and you are an inspiration – we're very fortunate to have your input. You have a way of making everything come into focus. From the heart….Dianne." I kept this note to remind me of the power of investing in people to help them learn and grow.

Do you believe that doors close because others are supposed to be open? Are you the type of person that looks for the rainbows after the storm? The bright light on this dark day was that I had to focus on the next day because I was delivering a keynote for a paper company during their yearly sales meeting. The president of the company initially told me the engagement was on a Thursday, so originally, I was going to take that day as mandatory PTO. He made a mistake and the meeting was on the same day as our department Holiday gathering. I'm sure it wasn't sending a good message that I was not attending the event, and was grateful for the opportunity to pursue my passion of speaking and provide financially for my family. The speech shifted my focus and it was the rainbow after the storm.

This experience also taught me that I need to be my own boss. I want to own my own time and choose the priorities and focus areas that I feel are important and that I feel God is calling me to do. What's challenging now is slowing down long enough to listen, to pray, to learn, to understand, to participate in the things that are important to God, my family and my career. In fact, after recently delivering a program to the Greensboro Merchant's Association called "5 Strategies to Transform Your Leadership and Enhance Your Business Results," I emailed the Director of the Business Center at our local community college and asked him if he would help me write a business plan. I told him, "I have short term and long term goals and key focus areas. I feel like I need a business plan to get me organized." We have a meeting scheduled next week! So how is your business going? Do you need a business plan or a professional development plan?

Are there relationships that empower you to do your job effectively or are they creating road blocks. Do you feel challenged & fulfilled in your leadership role or is it time to be a catalyst and create a positive change? Is it time to shift your focus?

Action Item

Ask someone in your organization whom you like, trust and respect to give you feedback on your leadership. Ask them to share: What is working, what's not working and what's missing from my leadership?

Proverbs 3:13

Blessed is the man who finds wisdom, the man who gains understanding.

10 CATALYST METHODOLOGY

Be the change you want to see in the world.
-Ghandi

This quote about change is one of my favorites. Change, for some people, is terrifying! Some professionals thrive on change, while others run from it as fast as they can. If you haven't read <u>Who Moved My Cheese</u> by Spencer Johnson, please order or download a copy after you read this chapter. It gives you a snapshot of how people deal with change.

During my year on the inside, the hospital's IT department was going through some changes and one of the directors asked if I would facilitate a program for them. I had conducted several team workshops for different departments to help improve communication, interpersonal skills and team performance.

When I arrived at the conference room, I realized I had forgotten to bring writing pens for the meeting. Since this was advertised as a lunch and learn program, I wasn't sure if everyone would bring a pen or pencil and I always liked to have a few as back up. I asked the first attendee who arrived to the room, "Do you have any extra pens?" The response was "No." So I turned to the next person who walked in and asked the same question. "If you are going to make people write during this meeting," this attendee said, "you are not going to have many participants."

The next person who walked in replied with some sort of sarcastic remark to which I replied, "I've decided whatever negativity comes my way today, I'm a OK with it, I've got my big girl panties on so I can deal with it today." She looked at me kind of strangely and said, "Let me go look in my office and see if I have any extra pens." You see there will be people in this life that will try to rain on your parade. I say, "Carry an umbrella!" Preferably one with great big yellow smiley faces! There is also a saying, "When life hands you lemons, make lemonade." (Thank you Mr. Carnegie.) I heard some say once, "When life hands you lemons, ask for Tequila and salt!" You pick, either one works!

Change happens in a millisecond. When the employee brought back the pens, she asked me, "Have you ever heard of this speaker?" The brochure she was holding was about a Navy Pilot who wrote a book and was teaching throughout the United States. This employee's tone was different; she had changed in a moment. She was inviting, personable, helpful. I asked if I could make a copy of the brochure and she said, "Oh, no problem, I'll do it for you." After the meeting, I thanked her for helping me and for sharing the information.

I went back to my office and began to read about this guy's philosophy, his methodology and I thought to myself, Merikay, what are you about? What do you do to help people develop? What's your methodology? I began to scratch out some words on a sheet of paper and four months later the Catalyst Methodology was created.

The Catalyst Methodology involves five core elements. The first one is Purpose. This is the "why factor": the mission, vision, business objective, or the goal.

The second element is People – the most critical asset in business is People! People need to be engaged, invested in for development, and work together as a high functioning team.

Work relationships need to be productive and thriving. There will be times when conflict exists. That's a good thing. Conflict means things are growing, changing, purging, shifting or sticking. When there is no conflict, there is no energy. It's not about singing Kumbaya all the time, or being fake or simply putting a smile on your face -- although a smile is a pretty good place to start! It's about finding joy in the work and in each other. Seeking to understand and relate to others even if you don't agree with them in some way. Most businesses can't run without people – and that's why investing in them is so important to the ongoing success of an organization.

The third element is Process. What customer service model is used? What delivery system of care does the organization follow? How streamlined is the work flow? You can have a great purpose and wonderful people, but if there is no system to follow and people are going in a million different directions, there is no consistency and business results will reflect the lack of systems.

The fourth element is Performance. How are results measured? How are individuals and teams recognized or appreciated for the efforts? What is the return on investment? How is the bottom line measured?

The fifth element is Communication. This is the glue that keeps it together or the solvent that dissolves things quickly. The ability to listen, understand, agree to disagree, respect, value, relate, question, debate (not argue or intimidate), inspire, encourage, strategize, plan, execute, hold accountable, coach, appreciate, improve, focus, serve - all of these are done through communication. Are you communicating the purpose of your organization in ways people understand? Are your people communicating well with each other? Do they understand how different personality types communicate in different ways? Do they understand how stress shifts communication? Are people spending too much time with emails and not enough time person to person. Communication is like toothpaste: once it's out of the tube, you can't put it back.

One person who is a powerful communicator is Tom Brittain, a Methodist preacher in Myrtle Beach, South Carolina. I met him when he spoke at our church. His daughter, Jan, was our senior pastor, so "Big Tom," as he was called, visited our church frequently to share inspirational messages. These are his Ten Rules for Living:

1. Don't ever fear the truth.
2. Don't act hastily. Always spend some quiet time in prayer before you make a big decision.
3. Find someone you respect and ask them to be your mentor.
4. Make peace with the fact that you cannot please everyone.
5. Over-dependence on self and under-dependence on God is the chief source of human misery.
6. Nothing you can see is permanent.
7. Always love and be faithful to your spouse.
8. Find a church and be active in it.
9. Become a tither. It will bless you.
10. Remember, in a single decision, a simple second or a single

act can make your life or destroy it. You can be the person God wants you to be.

As you review the list, what area spoke to you the most? Do you feel in your heart and mind that you are doing your best? Are you at a place where you need to do a little more for yourself or others? Where do you need to be a Catalyst for Change?

During our patient experience kick off sessions, I told each audience member that we needed to become a stronger team and we would accomplish that by treating each other better.

If people leading your organization are a dysfunctional team, chances are the dysfunction will continue in other departments. Patrick Lencioni's book, <u>The Five Dysfunctions of a Team</u>, describes this well. Here is a snapshot from his website at http://www.tablegroup.com/books/dysfunctions/

The Concept

The Five Dysfunctions of a Team outlines the root causes of politics and dysfunction on the teams where you work, and the keys to overcoming them. Counter to conventional wisdom, the causes of dysfunction are both identifiable and curable. However, they don't die easily. Making a team functional and cohesive requires levels of courage and discipline that many groups cannot seem to muster.

Dysfunction #1: Absence of Trust
The fear of being vulnerable with team members prevents the building of trust within the team.

Dysfunction #2: Fear of Conflict
The desire to preserve artificial harmony stifles the occurrence of productive ideological conflict.

Dysfunction #3: Lack of Commitment
The lack of clarity or buy-in prevents team members from making decisions they will stick to.

Dysfunction #4: Avoidance of Accountability
The need to avoid interpersonal discomfort prevents team members from holding one another accountable.

Dysfunction #5: Inattention to Results
The pursuit of individual goals and personal status erodes the focus on collective success.

Characteristics of High Performing Teams
Teams willing to address the five dysfunctions can experience the following benefits. High performing, cohesive teams:
- Are comfortable asking for help, admitting mistakes and limitations and take risks offering feedback
- Tap into one another's skills and experiences
- Avoid wasting time talking about the wrong issues and revisiting the same topics over and over again because of lack of buy-in
- Make higher quality decisions and accomplish more in less time and fewer resources
- Put critical topics on the table and have lively meetings
- Align the team around common objectives
- Retain star employees

I was familiar with this book prior to joining LRH, so I contacted the company to learn more about their programs. I secretly hoped that we would be able to use this book as a tool to acknowledge the dysfunction and chart a new course. When the reality hit me our organization suffered from all five dysfunctions, it was a tough moment for sure. What was more challenging was that some people in senior leadership didn't see it, and some knew it and didn't want to address it or feel safe to address the dysfunction.

Another person who is creating catalysts for change is the new president at LRH. I love it when team members share how he is inspiring them and making tough decisions to improve the organization. One of the directors shared with me that during a director/manager meeting each person stood up, introduced themselves and their departments. He then went around the room and addressed each person by name – nearly 120 people. He scheduled a one-on-one meeting with the people whose name he missed so he could get to get to know them.

In another meeting he asked the group "Who is the most important person in the organization?" Everyone responded, "the patient." He replied, "No, the most important person is you." WOW!!! When employees are engaged, care for each other and help each other, that care transfers to the patient and their family.

How would you rate your team? What levels of dysfunction exist? What characteristics of high performance teams exist? Have you surveyed your team to find out their perceptions, thoughts, and experiences?

An employee survey was conducted after my departure and several directors and the chief nursing officer lost their jobs. I admit, there was a moment when I thought, "What goes around, comes around." We have to be careful not to judge or have the 'get even' mindset. Also, one of the heaviest burdens we can carry is a grudge. I read that somewhere and have always remembered it.

It's important that we let go of the things and people that hurt us, and embrace where we are today. We need to forgive others and our own past mistakes so they don't have a stronghold on our present.

Here's the deal. There are good people in the world and bad people. There are also good people who do bad things. Let's try to hang out with as many good people that do good things as possible.

Let's also try to be the best person we can be by maximizing our emotional side – compassion, empathy, integrity, connectedness, courage, insight, self-awareness, and values. Let's be a difference maker.

I still have so much to learn about being a leader, improving my speaking, understanding how to serve my coaching clients better, and developing stronger content for my programs. I'm sure there are folks that would like to add to my list. Sometimes we will get it right, sometimes we will get it wrong. The key factor is that to keep trying.

What follows is an email a nurse coordinator sent to the all of the employees of the emergency department. At the time she was a participant in one of my professional development series classes and had made a commitment to improve relationships with co-workers. She read this email at our final session and it made a huge impact on her co-workers. She was a difference maker.

From: *Angela Dawson*
To: *ED MDs; ED PAs; ED Staff*
Date: *11/5/2013, 6:47 P.M.*
Subject: *A commitment*
CC: *Merikay Tillman*

To all ED Staff,

I have to write this while I am still in a sappy crappy state of mind. Sort of a Jerry Maguire state of being ☺.

I have spent the last two days at the Brenner's Pediatric Trauma Conference learning new things.

The last session today was survivor stories. Two children who were very badly hurt yet made it are doing well. Many a tear was shed by those who told the stories and those of us who heard them.

These particular children did not pass through our hands, but just the same I thought of all the ones that do and how important the work is that all of you do each and every day.

I want to apologize to you all for not spending enough time telling you that.

I think somewhere along the line of working on meeting trauma center criteria, I got so task focused that I have all too often let go of the people piece.

You are the people piece.

You and your hard work. How often we have asked you to adjust to yet another change or added task. Do more, work faster, do it this way – no, now do it this way.

We ask you to live in a Gumby land (I hope you know who Gumby is….) where you are ever pulled this way and that way.

Know this – I see you (Avatar like) and you matter. You save lives every day and you deserve better than I have given to this point.

So going forward in the touchy feely spirit of communicating from the heart and mind, I commit to you a different tone and approach. One that says I see you and know how hard you work and then says let's look at these things together and see what "we" can come up with to make it better. Feel free to remind me when I forget and my tone or approach slips back into nag, nag, nag ☺.

I truly see you and very deeply appreciate all that you do.

With deep respect,
Angela
Trauma Coordinator
Emergency Department

She so moved her colleagues at our final session in the professional development series, she was awarded recognition for being a difference maker among her peers. Being a catalyst for positive change impacts and enriches the lives of others.

This coordinator took a huge risk by sending this email. If you knew you couldn't fail, what would you do? Even if you did fail after you tried, so what? Would you try again? Or would you give up?

Speaking can be scary but even when I feel I didn't do my best, I try to improve elements for the next time. Each speech I give is customized for the group – it takes more time to prepare, but it's worth it in the end.

I delivered a program for the North Carolina Organization of Municipal Management Officers (OMPO) yesterday and was so inspired by the people that attended the meeting – they were so open with each other, dedicated to helping others and willing to learn. The program was called "Stepping Stones to Success" and highlighted three key areas: Business – passion and purpose; Life – positivity and power; and Relationships – poise and perspective. Stepping Stones is also my first book project which includes interviews from myself, Jack Canfield, Deepak Chopra, Dr. Denis Waitley and other experts sharing strategies to improve business, life and relationships. If you are interested in learning more, you can download an iBook format at www.coachmkay.com/SteppingStonesDownload. Often when you attend a conference you learn many things that make an impact or could make an impact. But when you get back to work, you don't know where to start. So I challenged the fifty or so leaders to walk away from their conference with two or three action items they wanted to implement over the next 90 days. I asked them to write down one thing they wanted to do differently on a note card and to place it on their computer, in their portfolio, in their car...to put it someplace where they could see it every day for at least four weeks. If we keep a topic top of mind and focus energy and activity towards that goal, it increases the likelihood of success, of behavior change. The quote I closed the session with was by Arthur Ashe: "Start where you are. Use what you have. Do what you can." Are you ready to be a Catalyst for Change?

It's been close to one year since I finished my year on the inside. Challenges can be opportunities in disguise. Consider this story from Stepping Stones to Success: a man was fired from a home improvement store so he took his ideas and founded Home Depot. *What challenges have you experienced that you can turn into opportunities? Choose to be a Catalyst for Change to create success in how you communicate, lead and serve others.*

Action Item

Create a "ME" file for notes, cards, or emails that you receive from people to inspire you during those challenging moments that may be opportunities.

Romans 12:8

If it is encouraging, let him encourage; if it is contributing to the needs of others, let him give generously; if it is leadership, let him govern diligently; if it is showing mercy, let him do it cheerfully.

AUTHOR

Merikay is a bundle of energy and her humorous spirit is captivating. She's also a giving and committed caregiver who has helped professionals grow and improve for over 15 years. Merikay Hunt Tillman, M.S. is the Founder & CEO of COACH MKay Companies, LLC, based in Greensboro, North Carolina, an organization that creates catalysts for change to transform teams & impact the patient & customer experience. Her educational background includes a B.S. from UNC-Chapel Hill, and a master's degree from NC A&T State University in Human Resource Counseling. Merikay served as a multi-course certified Dale Carnegie® instructor for over 15 years. She is a nationally awarded professional speaker and has delivered over 1,000 customized presentations to audiences including Ralph Lauren, BB&T, Volvo Business Services, Good Samaritan Hospital, Carrier, MGMA, AADOM & the Glen L. Hunt, DDS Dental Society. Visit www.coachmkay.com for sign up for FREE resources, additional client listings and testimonials. Follow us on Facebook @COACH MKay or connect via LinkedIn – Merikay Tillman. To invite Merikay to speak to your organization or create a customized program for your team, please call Merikay direct: (336) 255-3273 or connect through coachmkay.com.

End Notes
1. Dusty Staub, Leadership International
   http://www.youtube.com/watch?v=I0JbpP_u-Tube, p. 4.

2. J. Mansoor, M.D., Sept. 5, 2012
   https://www.youtube.com/watch?v=wi8QutoYycg, p. 4.

3. Nancy Friedman,
   www.telephonedoctor.com/userfiles/WorkBooks/TD11, p. 7.

4. Peter Bregman, 18 Minutes, (New York, Business Plus, Hachette
   Book Group, 2011), http://peterbregman.com/18-minutes, p.
   9.

5. Joyce Meyer, Living Beyond Your Feelings, (New York, Faith
   Words, Hachette Book Group, 2011),
   http://www.joycemeyer.org, p. 14.

6. Deepak Chopra, Jack Canfield, Merikay Tillman, Dr. Denis
   Waitley and a compilation from other business leaders,
   Stepping Stones to Success, (Sevierville, Tenn. ISN Works and
   Insight Publishing, 2011), p. 25.

7. John C. Maxwell, Leadership 101, (Nashville, Thomas Nelson
   Publishers, 2002), p. 32.

8. "The Power of Teamwork" from Simple Truths, featuring the
   Blue Angels fighter pilots.
   http://play.simpletruths.com/movie/the-power-of-
   teamwork/store. p.33.

9. Bruce Wilkinson, The Prayer of Jabez, (Sisters, Ore. Multnomah
   Publishing, 2000), p.35.

10. Sweeney Healthcare,
    http://sweeneyhealthcareenterprises.com/. P 43.

11. Quint Studer, www.studergroup.com, p.46

12. The Lion King, http://movies.disney.com/the-lion-king, p. 55

13.   Dale Carnegie, How to Win Friends and Influence People, (New York, Simon and Schuster, 1936), p. 62

14. Youngey Mingyur Rinpoche, The Joy of Living, (New York, Harmony Books, affiliate of Penguin Random House Books, 2007), p. 62

15. Cleveland Clinic, http://my.clevelandclinic.org/ p.74

16. Dr. Rick Brinkman and Dr. Rick Kirschner, Dealing with People You Can't Stand, (McGraw Hill, New York, 1994), p. 85.

17. Dr. Gary Chapman and Dr. Paul White, The Five Languages of Appreciation in the Workplace, (Chicago, Northfield Publishing, 2011), p. 89.

18. "Overwhelmed America: Why Don't We Use Our Paid Time Off? http://www.huffingtonpost.com/arianna-huffington/paid-vacation-days_b_5693225.html, p. 100.

19. Melody Beattie, Codependent No More, (Center City, Minn., Hazelden, 1986). p.101.

20. Dale Carnegie, How to Stop Worrying and Start Living, (Great Britain, Richard Clay, The Chaucer Press, 1948) p. 102.

21. Raymond Hull and Laurence J. Peter, The Peter Principle, (New York, W. Morrow, 1969), p. 108.

22. T. Falcon Napier, Institute for Production Tension, http://www.productivetension.com/, p. 109.

44323201R00076

Made in the USA
Middletown, DE
03 June 2017